THE BATTLE BETWEEN

PERCEPTION AND REALITY

Two Faces OF MISUNDERSTOOD MINDS

DR. KINDALL M. BUNDY, QMHP, CDP

Dr. Kindall M. Bundy.
Published by Fusion Dynamics & You, LLC

ISBN: 978-1-960973-47-4

Disclaimer

This book is intended for educational and informational purposes only. It is not a substitute for professional diagnosis, treatment, or medical advice. The theories, interpretations, and examples presented reflect the author's perspectives and research and are not meant to provide definitive clinical guidance.

If you or someone you know is struggling with symptoms related to narcissism, schizophrenia, dementia, or any mental health condition, please seek evaluation and support from a licensed mental health professional or qualified healthcare provider.

Any resemblance of case examples in this book to actual individuals, living or deceased, is coincidental or based on composite experiences designed to illustrate key concepts.

The author and publisher disclaim any liability for actions taken or not taken based on the information provided in this text.

Contents

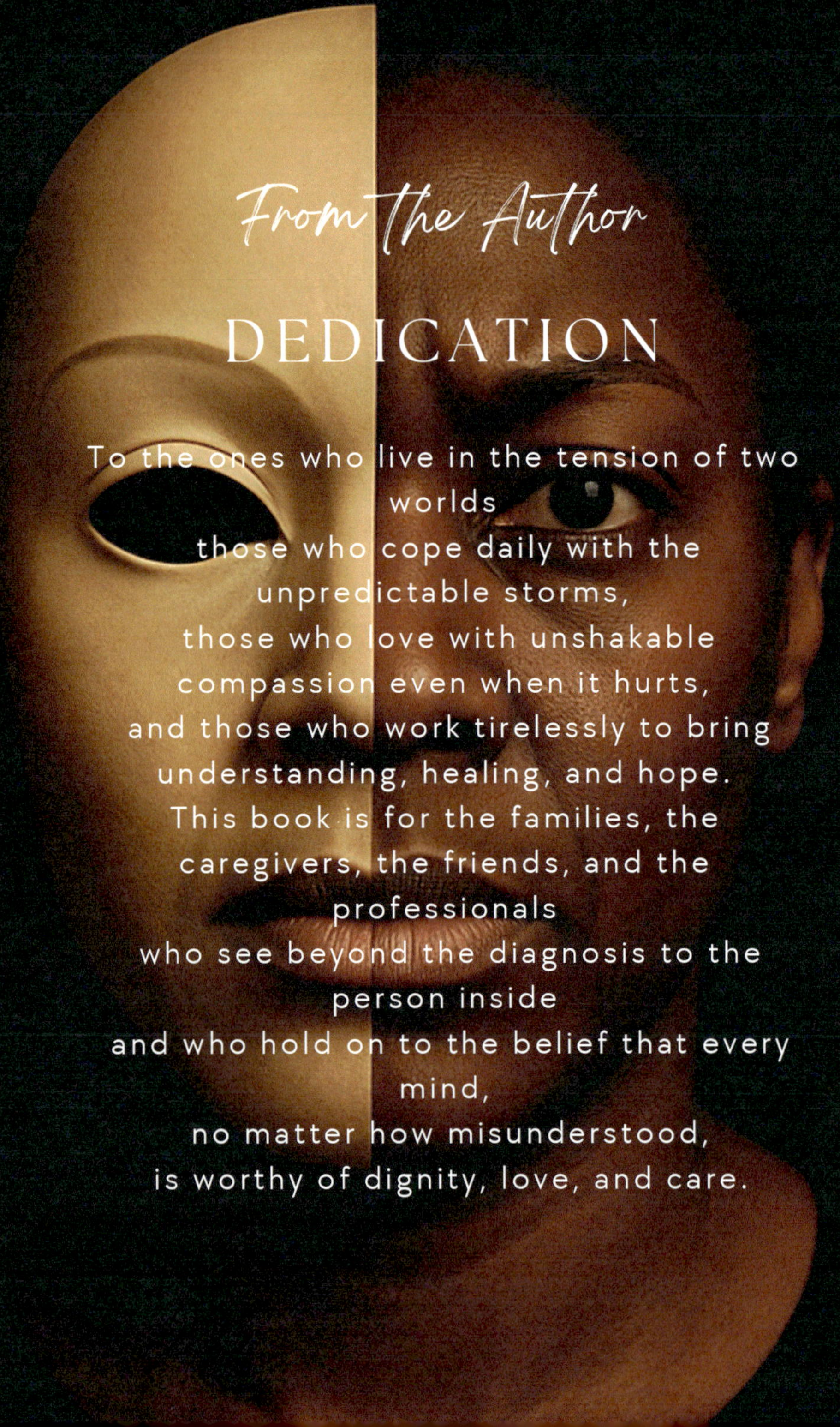

From the Author

DEDICATION

To the ones who live in the tension of two worlds
those who cope daily with the unpredictable storms,
those who love with unshakable compassion even when it hurts,
and those who work tirelessly to bring understanding, healing, and hope.
This book is for the families, the caregivers, the friends, and the professionals
who see beyond the diagnosis to the person inside
and who hold on to the belief that every mind,
no matter how misunderstood,
is worthy of dignity, love, and care.

INTRODUCTION

Torn Between the Two

The human mind is a labyrinth of mirrors, each reflection both familiar and distorted, each angle shifting depending on who is looking. Nowhere is this more evident than in the blurred boundaries of narcissism and schizophrenia, two conditions that, while distinct in the diagnostic manuals, often collide in practice and perception.

To the untrained eye, the narcissist and the schizophrenic can appear alike: both speak of realities that others cannot see, both behave in ways that distance them from their communities, and both seem to live in worlds set apart from the ordinary. Clinicians, families, and even patients themselves often wrestle with the same haunting question: Is this grandiosity or is it delusion? Is this manipulation or is it a hallucination?

This confusion is not accidental. At the root of both disorders lies fantasy. For the narcissist, fantasy is a self-crafted empire: a world where they are adored, superior, and untouchable.

For the schizophrenic, fantasy arrives uninvited, breaking through perception in the form of voices, visions, or fragmented beliefs that feel more real than reality itself. Both conditions stretch the boundary between what is imagined and what is true, and both can trap a person in a state where escape feels impossible.

Yet, while psychiatry has traditionally held narcissism and schizophrenia in separate categories, one a personality disorder, the other a psychotic disorder, this book dares to ask a deeper question: What if they are not as separate as we believe?

I propose a new theory: that narcissism and schizophrenia are not only behavioral diagnoses with overlapping features, but also potential gateways to a further dimension of mental decline and dementia.

If narcissism's fantasies and schizophrenia's delusions go unchecked, they may not merely disturb the present; they may erode the very memory of reality itself. In this sense, dementia becomes the "dimension of no return," the final stage where the mind, long immersed in distorted realities, loses its capacity to anchor itself to truth or memory.

This theory does not suggest that all narcissists will develop schizophrenia, nor that all individuals with schizophrenia will progress to dementia. Rather, it highlights the fragile thread that runs through each condition: the mind's reliance on fantasy to survive and the cost when fantasy is allowed to dominate.

In the chapters that follow, we will explore how these conditions mirror and diverge, what parts of the brain are most affected, and how fantasy, whether it is a grandiose illusion, a hallucinated voice, or a fragmented memory, can pull the mind into deeper dimensions. By tracing this path, we begin to understand how a person torn between the two may, without intervention, slip further into a state from which return is no longer possible.

This book is not only about diagnoses. It is about the fragile boundaries of the human mind, about how imagination can heal or destroy, and about why compassion, accurate understanding, and early intervention matter more than ever.

CHAPTER 1

Two Faces of Misunderstood Minds

Two Faces of Misunderstood Minds

CHAPTER 1

The human mind is an intricate landscape, layered with perception, memory, fantasy, and identity. At its best, this landscape fuels creativity, empathy, and resilience. At its most fragile, it fractures into patterns that others label with clinical names and diagnoses designed to capture what is seen on the surface. Narcissism and schizophrenia are two such names. Though often treated as opposites in psychiatric manuals, one lodged in the realm of personality, the other in the realm of psychosis, when observed closely, they reveal startling overlaps.

This chapter explores those overlaps. To do so, we must first understand each face of these misunderstood minds: narcissism, with its grandiose surface and fragile undercurrent; and schizophrenia, with its haunting distortions of perception and thought. Then we will look at how these diagnoses, built primarily on behavioral observation, sometimes blur into one another, creating the risk of misdiagnosis and the deeper cost of misunderstanding.

Defining Narcissism: The Mask of Grandeur

Narcissistic Personality Disorder (NPD) is defined in the Diagnostic and Statistical Manual of Mental Disorders, Fifth Edition (DSM-5) as a pervasive pattern of grandiosity, need for admiration, and lack of empathy, beginning in early adulthood and present in a variety of contexts. At least five of nine criteria must be met for a clinical diagnosis.

The hallmarks include:

- A grandiose sense of self-importance.
- Preoccupation with fantasies of unlimited success, power, brilliance, beauty, or ideal love.
- Belief in being special and unique, understandable only by high-status people or institutions.
- Need for excessive admiration.
- A sense of entitlement.
- Interpersonally exploitative behaviors.
- Lack of empathy.
- Envy of others or belief that others envy them.
- Arrogant, haughty behaviors or attitudes.

Yet beneath these behaviors lies something easily overlooked: the narcissist's reliance on fantasy. The imagined world, whether it is one of boundless power, perfect love, or unquestioned superiority, provides insulation against deep insecurity, shame, or emptiness. For some, these fantasies are conscious daydreams; for others, they become so embedded that they are experienced as reality. This reliance on fantasy is precisely where narcissism begins to echo the terrain of schizophrenia.

Defining Schizophrenia: The Shattered Mirror

Schizophrenia, in contrast, is classified not as a personality disorder but as a psychotic disorder. It is marked by disruptions in thought, perception, and sense of reality. The DSM-5 outlines its key features:

- Delusions (fixed false beliefs).
- Hallucinations (sensory perceptions without external stimulus).
- Disorganized speech (frequent derailment or incoherence).
- Grossly disorganized or catatonic behavior.
- Negative symptoms (diminished emotional expression, avolition).

At least two of these, with at least one being delusions, hallucinations, or disorganized speech, must be present for a significant period.

Like narcissism, schizophrenia also centers on fantasy but in a different register. Here, fantasy is not chosen or cultivated as a shield but intrudes uninvited. The mind becomes both architect and captive of realities others cannot see. A man may hear the voice of a long-dead relative. A woman may believe she is being monitored by secret agents. A student may become convinced that their thoughts are being broadcast over radio waves.

The difference between narcissism's fantasies and schizophrenia's delusions appears obvious: one inflates the self, the other distorts the world. Yet when we step closer, we see they are not so easily disentangled.

The Diagnostic Frameworks: Walls That Blur

On paper, psychiatry builds clear walls between these disorders. Narcissism is grouped with other personality disorders—enduring patterns of inner experience and behavior that deviate from expectations of the individual's culture. Schizophrenia is grouped with psychotic disorders marked by fundamental distortions in thinking and perception.

But the practical application of these frameworks relies heavily on behavioral observation. A clinician does not look directly into the brain; instead, they listen to speech, watch behaviors, and record what is seen. A narcissist boasting of being chosen by God and destined to lead the world may sound eerily similar to a schizophrenic describing a divine mission guided by voices.

A person with schizophrenia who insists they are superior, misunderstood by ordinary people, may echo the entitlement of narcissism.

What begins as a neat separation on paper becomes tangled in practice. Both diagnoses orbit around fantasy, both distort how the self is experienced, and both challenge the boundaries of reality.

Behavioral Overlaps That Confuse Diagnosis

1. Grandiosity vs. Delusion of Grandeur
    - The narcissist claims superiority because it maintains their fragile self-esteem.
    - The schizophrenic may hold a delusional belief of superiority as part of psychosis.
    - From the outside, both insist: I am chosen, special, above others. Distinguishing whether this is a defensive fantasy (narcissism) or a psychotic delusion (schizophrenia) is not always straightforward.
2. Suspicion and Paranoia
    - Narcissists may interpret others' actions as threats to their superiority, reacting with suspicion.
    - Schizophrenics often experience persecutory delusions, believing they are being followed, monitored, or harmed.
    - Both create strained relationships built on mistrust.
3. Empathy Deficits
    - Narcissists often lack empathy because their attention is consumed by self-preservation.
    - Schizophrenics may appear unempathic because negative symptoms blunt emotional expression.

In either case, family and caregivers describe them as "unable to feel what others feel."

4. Identity Distortion

- Narcissists may present a false self, constructed from fantasy.
- Schizophrenics may lose boundaries of self altogether, convinced their thoughts are controlled by others.
- In both, the question "Who am I?" becomes fragile, unstable, and difficult to ground.

5. Social Isolation

- Narcissists isolate because others cannot live up to their expectations.
- Schizophrenics isolate due to mistrust, hallucinations, or negative symptoms.
- Both may appear aloof, detached, or resistant to connection.

Case Vignette: The Pastor's Son

Consider James, the son of a pastor in a small community. At nineteen, he begins to tell friends he has been chosen to lead a great revival. He describes visions of angels, dreams that foretell disasters, and a sense that God whispers instructions directly into his mind. His parents, proud of his passion, encourage him. However, his peers begin to notice that his stories become increasingly elaborate. He claims that classmates who doubt him are secretly agents of Satan. He stops attending classes, insisting that his divine mission is more important.

When James is taken to a clinic, two psychiatrists disagree. One diagnoses schizophrenia: auditory hallucinations, persecutory delusions, and functional decline. Another suspect of narcissistic personality disorder: a deep need to be seen as special, fantasies of unlimited power, and disdain for ordinary obligations.

Which is it? The truth may be both or neither because the categories themselves are built on behaviors that overlap in the realm of fantasy.

The Role of Culture in Misdiagnosis

Cultural context complicates the picture even further. In some cultures, hearing the voices of ancestors is considered spiritual, not psychotic. In others, public claims of grandeur may be interpreted as confidence, not narcissism. Diagnostic manuals, built largely on Western frameworks, risk pathologizing what may be culturally normative or missing what is pathological beneath cultural language.

This means a narcissist in one culture may be seen as visionary in another; a schizophrenic in one culture may be honored as a mystic in another. The overlap between narcissism and schizophrenia is therefore not just clinical but cultural, shaped by what societies deem as acceptable fantasy.

The Cost of Misdiagnosis

The stakes of confusion are high.

- For the narcissist misdiagnosed as schizophrenic, they may be prescribed antipsychotics, facing unnecessary side effects without addressing their core vulnerabilities.
- For the schizophrenic misdiagnosed as narcissist: they may be sent to therapy alone, with no medication to stabilize psychosis, leading to deterioration.
- For families: misdiagnosis means years of confusion, guilt, and ineffective care.

At the core of both is a single truth: fantasy is central to each disorder, and fantasy is difficult to measure. What looks like arrogance may be delusion. What looks like psychosis may be defense.

The line between them, thin as it is, carries profound consequences.

Fantasy as the Meeting Ground

When stripped to their essence, both narcissism and schizophrenia pivot on the question of reality versus fantasy.

- Narcissists construct fantasies to inflate and protect the self.
- Schizophrenics experience fantasy as an uncontrollable invasion of reality.

In both, fantasy becomes a second dimension, pulling the person away from consensus reality. This shared dependence on fantasy creates the illusion of similarity and the risk of conflation.

But it also opens a new lens: instead of rigid categories, perhaps these conditions can be seen as different ways the mind uses fantasy to survive one intentional, one imposed.

The Clinical Overlaps: Where Labels Fail

The neat categories of narcissism and schizophrenia collapse quickly in practice. Clinicians and families alike often encounter symptoms that defy binary labeling. A young woman who insists she is destined for greatness: is she cloaked in narcissistic fantasy or lost in a schizophrenic delusion? A man who refuses to trust anyone, convinced they are envious of him: is this narcissistic paranoia or psychotic persecution?

The overlaps fall into several domains, each of which deepens the diagnostic fog.

1. **Speech and Thought Patterns**
Both narcissistic individuals and those with schizophrenia may speak in ways that perplex others.

- Narcissists often exhibit circumstantiality; their speech circles back repeatedly to their own brilliance, grievances, or fantasies of success.
- Schizophrenics often exhibit loosening of associations, sentences may jump in illogical directions, yet still circle themes of self-importance, threat, or mystical significance.

The result for the listener can feel similar: a sense of being pulled into someone else's inner world, where ordinary conversational rules no longer apply.

2. **Self-Reference and Persecution**
A hallmark of narcissism is the belief that everything is about them, compliments, criticisms, successes, and failures. Schizophrenia shares a similar thread through ideas of reference beliefs that neutral events (a song on the radio, a glance from a stranger) are directed at them personally.

In both conditions, ordinary reality becomes personalized to the extreme. A narcissist might say, "The meeting failed because they're jealous of me." A schizophrenic might insist, "The newscaster on TV is sending me secret warnings." The difference is a subtle one, grounded in insecurity, the other in psychotic distortion, but the surface similarity is striking.

3. **Emotional Dysregulation**

- Narcissists may lash out in rage when their fantasies are challenged.

- Schizophrenics may become agitated or fearful when hallucinations or delusions overwhelm them.

In both, emotional outbursts seem disproportionate to external events, leading families to describe them as unpredictable, volatile, or frightening.

The Clinical Overlaps: Where Labels Fail

The neat categories of narcissism and schizophrenia collapse quickly in practice. Clinicians and families alike often encounter symptoms that defy binary labeling. A young woman who insists she is destined for greatness: is she cloaked in narcissistic fantasy or lost in a schizophrenic delusion? A man who refuses to trust anyone, convinced they are envious of him: is this narcissistic paranoia or psychotic persecution?

The overlaps fall into several domains, each of which deepens the diagnostic fog.

1. **Speech and Thought Patterns**

Both narcissistic individuals and those with schizophrenia may speak in ways that perplex others.

- Narcissists often exhibit circumstantiality, their speech circles back repeatedly to their own brilliance, grievances, or fantasies of success.
- Schizophrenics often exhibit loosening of associations—sentences may jump in illogical directions, yet still circle around themes of self-importance, threat, or mystical significance.

The result for the listener can feel similar: a sense of being pulled into someone else's inner world, where ordinary conversational rules no longer apply.

2. **Self-Reference and Persecution**

A hallmark of narcissism is the belief that everything is about compliments, criticisms, successes, and failures. Schizophrenia shares a similar thread through ideas of reference beliefs that neutral events (a song on the radio, a glance from a stranger) are directed at them personally.

In both conditions, ordinary reality becomes personalized to the extreme. A narcissist might say, "The meeting failed because they're jealous of me." A schizophrenic might insist, "The newscaster on TV is sending me secret warnings." The difference is a subtle one grounded in insecurity, the other in psychotic distortion, but the surface similarity is striking.

3. **Emotional Dysregulation**

- Narcissists may lash out in rage when their fantasies are challenged.
- Schizophrenics may become agitated or fearful when hallucinations or delusions overwhelm them.

In both, emotional outbursts seem disproportionate to external events, leading families to describe them as unpredictable, volatile, or frightening.

4. **Social Disruption**

Both disorders dismantle relationships.

- Narcissists exploit or discard those who fail to mirror their fantasies.
- Schizophrenics withdraw or alienate others under the weight of mistrust or incoherence.

In practice, both may end up isolated misunderstood by peers, avoided by family, or marginalized by society.

5. **The Problem of Insight**

Insight, the ability to recognize that one has a mental health condition is often impaired in both.

- Narcissists rarely admit to being narcissistic; it threatens their self-image.
- Schizophrenics may deny their delusions or hallucinations are symptoms; to them, these experiences are real.

Thus, both resist treatment, not necessarily from stubbornness, but from the genuine belief that nothing is wrong.

CHAPTER 2

The Role of Fantasy

The Role of Fantasy

CHAPTER 2

The Worlds We Create, The Worlds That Create Us

Fantasy is one of the most powerful functions of the human mind. It is the birthplace of creativity, innovation, and resilience. It allows a child to imagine possibility, an artist to bring vision to life, and a survivor to mentally escape circumstances that feel unbearable. Fantasy, in its healthiest form, is not pathology, it is protection, adaptation, and expansion.

But like all powerful tools, fantasy exists on a spectrum. When regulated, it enhances reality. When unchecked, it begins to replace it. This chapter explores what happens when fantasy moves from a supportive mental function to a dominant force, when it becomes the lens through which a person interprets themselves and the world. It is within this shift that we begin to see the convergence of narcissism and schizophrenia. Though these conditions are often separated by diagnostic boundaries, both rely heavily on fantasy, one constructing it, the other experiencing it as imposed reality.

To understand this connection, we must first examine how fantasy operates within narcissism.

Narcissistic Fantasies of Grandeur: The Constructed Self

At the core of narcissism lies a paradox: an inflated sense of self built upon a fragile foundation.

The narcissistic individual does not simply believe they are superior, they must believe it. This belief is not optional; it is a psychological necessity.
Fantasy becomes the architecture of this necessity.
Narcissistic fantasies often center around themes of:

- Unlimited success
- Power and influence
- Idealized love or admiration
- Exceptional intelligence or beauty
- Destiny or uniqueness
- These fantasies are not fleeting daydreams. They are internal narratives, rehearsed and reinforced until they feel indistinguishable from truth.

A narcissistic individual may imagine themselves as the smartest person in the room, even when evidence suggests otherwise. They may believe they are destined for greatness despite repeated failures. They may rewrite past experiences to maintain a sense of superiority, erasing moments that threaten their self-image.

This is not simply arrogance. It is **psychological survival**.

The False Self and the Fantasy Identity

Psychoanalytic theory, particularly the work of Otto Kernberg and Heinz Kohut, describes narcissism as the development of a false self, a constructed identity designed to protect against deep feelings of inadequacy or shame.
Fantasy fuels this false self.

Instead of confronting vulnerability, the narcissistic mind builds an alternate identity, one that is flawless, admired, and immune to criticism. Over time, this identity becomes the dominant self-experience.

The individual no longer feels like they are pretending; they feel like they are revealing their "true" greatness.

Yet this greatness is sustained not by reality, but by constant reinforcement:

- External validation (praise, admiration)
- Internal narratives (self-talk reinforcing superiority)
- Reinterpretation of events (turning failures into perceived successes)

Fantasy, in this sense, is both shield and scaffolding. It protects the individual while also holding up the structure of their identity.

Fantasy as Emotional Regulation

For the narcissistic individual, fantasy is not just about identity, it is about regulating emotion.

When faced with:

- Criticism → fantasy restores superiority
- Rejection → fantasy creates imagined admiration
- Failure → fantasy reframes outcome as misunderstood success

This process happens quickly, often unconsciously. The mind shifts from painful reality to protective fantasy before the individual fully experiences the emotional impact.

In this way, fantasy acts as a buffer against distress.

However, this buffering comes at a cost. Each time fantasy overrides reality, the individual becomes more dependent on it. Reality becomes less tolerable, and fantasy becomes more necessary.

This is the beginning of the trap.

When Fantasy Becomes Rigidity

In healthy individuals, fantasy is flexible. It can be engaged and disengaged. One can dream, imagine, and then return to reality without confusion.

In narcissism, fantasy becomes rigid.

The individual may:

- Reject feedback that contradicts their self-image
- Dismiss evidence that challenges their beliefs
- Surround themselves with people who reinforce their fantasies
- Become hostile when their narrative is questioned

At this stage, fantasy is no longer a tool, it is a requirement.

The line between imagination and belief begins to blur.

And this is where narcissism begins to approach the territory of schizophrenia.

Schizophrenic Delusions and Hallucinations: The Imposed Reality

While narcissism constructs fantasy, schizophrenia experiences it as intrusion.

The schizophrenic individual does not choose their alternate reality. It arrives uninvited, often overwhelming, and deeply convincing.

The defining features include:

- *Delusions:* fixed false beliefs that persist despite evidence
- *Hallucinations:* sensory experiences without external stimuli
- *Disorganized thinking:* fragmented or illogical thought patterns

Unlike narcissistic fantasy, which often centers on self-enhancement, schizophrenic delusions may include:

- Persecution (being watched, targeted, or harmed)
- Control (thoughts being inserted or removed)
- Grandiosity (special powers or divine missions)

- Reference (belief that external events are directed at them)

These experiences are not imagined in the casual sense, they are perceived as reality.

The Experience of Hallucination

To understand schizophrenia, one must understand the intensity of hallucination.

A voice heard during a hallucination is not experienced as "thinking." It is experienced as hearing. The brain processes it through the same sensory pathways as external sound.

The individual may hear:

- Commands ("Do this." "Don't trust them.")
- Commentary ("You are being watched.")
- Conversations between voices

These voices can be comforting, critical, or terrifying. Regardless of tone, they are convincing.

The individual is not choosing to believe they, are responding to what feels real.

Delusion as Meaning-Making

Delusions often serve a purpose: they organize the chaos of hallucinations into a coherent narrative.

If a person hears voices, they may develop a belief system to explain them:

- "I am being tested."
- "I have a special mission."
- "There are forces controlling me."

In this way, delusion is not random, it is meaning making under distortion.

Just as narcissistic fantasy construct's identity, schizophrenic delusion constructs explanation.

Both are attempts by the mind to make sense of experience.

Overlap in Grandiosity

One of the most striking overlaps between narcissism and schizophrenia is grandiosity.

A narcissist may believe:
"I am exceptional. Others are beneath me."
A schizophrenic individual may believe:
"I have been chosen for a divine purpose."
In both cases, the individual occupies a position of special significance.
The difference lies in origin:

- Narcissism → internally constructed fantasy
- Schizophrenia → externally perceived reality

Yet to the observer, both may appear identical.

Fantasy as Escape

At this point, a pattern begins to emerge: fantasy, whether constructed or imposed, serves as escape.

- Escape from inadequacy (narcissism)
- Escape from confusion or fear (schizophrenia)
- Escape from emotional pain (both)

Fantasy offers relief. It creates a space where the individual feels:

- Powerful instead of powerless
- Certain instead of confused
- Important instead of insignificant

This relief is not trivial. It is deeply reinforcing.
The brain begins to associate fantasy with safety.

The Turning Point: When Escape Becomes Entrapment

The danger of fantasy is not its existence, it is its dominance.
When fantasy becomes the primary way of engaging with the world:

- Reality feels threatening
- Relationships become strained
- Insight diminishes
- Functioning declines

What once served as protection becomes limitation.

The narcissistic individual becomes trapped in a self-image that cannot adapt.
The schizophrenic individual becomes trapped in a reality they cannot escape.

Both are confined, just in different ways.

A Shared Psychological Mechanism

Though their origins differ, narcissistic fantasy and schizophrenic delusion share a common mechanism:
They replace external validation of reality with internal conviction.
In healthy functioning, reality is negotiated:

- We test our beliefs against others
- We adjust when proven wrong
- We remain flexible

In both narcissism and schizophrenia, this process breaks down.
The individual relies on internal experience over external feedback.
This is the beginning of detachment from consensus reality.

Case Reflection: Two Stories, One Pattern

Consider two individuals:
Elena, who believes she is destined to be a world-renowned figure, dismissing all criticism as jealousy.

Marcus, who believes he has been chosen to communicate with unseen forces guiding humanity.
Their stories differ in origin, but their experiences converge:

- Both feel special
- Both resist contradiction
- Both live in realities others cannot fully access

Fantasy is not inherently dangerous. It is one of the mind's most remarkable abilities. But when it becomes the dominant force, when it replaces rather than enhances reality, it begins to reshape identity, perception, and behavior.
In narcissism, fantasy builds a world where the self is untouchable.
In schizophrenia, fantasy builds a world where reality itself is unstable.
Both offer escape.
Both carry risk.

And both set the stage for a deeper question, one that we will explore in the next section:
What happens when the mind can no longer return?

The Trap Within the Escape

Fantasy begins as a doorway, but for many, it becomes a room with no exit.

In both narcissism and schizophrenia, fantasy does not remain a passive mental activity. It evolves. It strengthens. It begins to organize thought, emotion, and identity. What was once a coping mechanism becomes a primary operating system of the mind.

To understand how this happens, we must explore the mechanics of entrapment, how fantasy reinforces itself, how it reshapes identity, and how, over time, it can consume the individual entirely.

The Reinforcement Loop: How Fantasy Feeds Itself

The human brain is wired for reinforcement. Behaviors and thoughts that reduce distress or increase pleasure are repeated. This is the foundation of learning, habit formation, and survival.

Fantasy, when it provides relief, becomes subject to this same system.

Step 1: Emotional Trigger

The process often begins with discomfort:

- Shame
- Rejection
- Fear
- Confusion
- Loneliness

These emotional states are difficult to tolerate. The mind seeks relief.

Step 2: Fantasy Activation

The individual shifts—consciously or unconsciously—into fantasy:

- The narcissist imagines admiration, success, or superiority.
- The schizophrenic experiences hallucinations or constructs delusional meaning.

In that moment, distress is reduced.

Step 3: Relief and Reward

Relief is not neutral, it is rewarding. The brain releases dopamine, reinforcing the mental shift.

The message becomes:

"This helped. Do it again."

Step 4: Repetition

Over time, the mind learns to default to fantasy:

- Faster activation
- Stronger belief
- Greater emotional dependence

What began as occasional escape becomes habitual response.

Step 5: Entrenchment

Eventually, fantasy is no longer optional. It becomes the preferred and then required state.

At this stage:

- Reality feels insufficient or threatening
- Fantasy feels necessary for emotional survival
- Contradictions are rejected or distorted

The loop is complete.

Narcissism and the Reinforcement of Grandeur

For the narcissistic individual, this loop centers on self-enhancement.

Each time reality challenges their self-image, fantasy restores it:

- A failed opportunity becomes "they couldn't handle my greatness"
- Criticism becomes "they're jealous"
- Rejection becomes "they're not worthy of me"

This process is not random, it is systematic.

Over time, the narcissistic individual builds a closed system of belief, where:

- Every event reinforces their superiority
- Every contradiction is reinterpreted
- Every relationship becomes a mirror or a threat

The result is a self-sustaining identity, built almost entirely on fantasy.

Schizophrenia and the Reinforcement of Delusion

In schizophrenia, the loop operates differently, but leads to similar entrenchment.

The individual experiences hallucinations or unusual perceptions. These experiences are confusing, often frightening. The mind attempts to organize them through delusion.

For example:

- Hearing a voice → "Someone is speaking to me"
- Feeling watched → "I am being monitored"
- Emotional intensity → "This must mean something important"

Once a delusional explanation is formed, it provides structure.

And structure brings relief. Even if the belief is distressing, it is less distressing than chaos. So, the brain reinforces it.

The Illusion of Control vs. the Loss of Control

This is where the two conditions diverge most sharply, and yet still converge.

- The narcissist experiences fantasy as control:
- "I shape my reality. I define who I am."
- The schizophrenic experiences fantasy as intrusion:
- "Reality is happening to me. I cannot control it."

Yet over time, both lose flexibility.

The narcissist becomes controlled by the need to maintain the fantasy.

The schizophrenic becomes controlled by the inability to escape it.

Both are trapped.

Identity Collapse: When the Self Becomes the Fantasy

One of the most profound consequences of prolonged fantasy immersion is identity collapse.

In Narcissism: The Self Becomes the Performance

The narcissistic individual begins with a constructed identity, but over time, that construction replaces the authentic self.

They no longer ask:

- "Who am I?"

Instead, they live as:

- "Who I must be."

The original self—vulnerable, uncertain, human—becomes inaccessible.

What remains is the performance:

- Confident
- Superior
- Unquestionable

But beneath the performance is fragility. Without the fantasy, there is no stable identity.

In Schizophrenia: The Self Becomes Fragmented

In schizophrenia, identity collapse takes a different form.

Instead of a constructed self, there is a fragmented self:

- Thoughts feel external
- Emotions feel disconnected
- Identity boundaries blur

The individual may ask:

- "Are these my thoughts?"
- "Is this real?"
- "Who am I in this experience?"

The self is no longer anchored.

The Shared Outcome: Loss of Grounded Identity

Though the paths differ, the result converges:
Both individuals lose a stable, grounded sense of self.

- One replaces it with fantasy
- The other loses it within distortion

In both, identity becomes unstable, dependent on internal narratives rather than external reality.

Case Study 1: The Influencer

Tanya, 31, builds a strong online presence. She presents herself as a highly successful entrepreneur, though in reality, her business struggles financially. When followers question her claims, she blocks them. She surrounds herself with affirming voices and begins to believe her own narrative.

Over time:

- Her online persona becomes her identity
- Real-life relationships deteriorate
- Financial instability increases

When confronted by family, she reacts with rage:
"You're just trying to bring me down."

Tanya is not lying in the traditional sense; she is living within a reinforced fantasy.

Case Study 2: The Veteran

Darius, 40, returns from military service. He begins hearing voices that sound like former commanders. At first, he questions them. Over time, he accepts them as real.

The voices guide his actions:

- "Stay alert."
- "Don't trust them."
- "You're still on duty."

Darius constructs a belief system:

"I have been chosen to remain vigilant. Others don't understand."
This belief reduces confusion but isolates him from reality.
His family sees withdrawal. He sees purpose.

Case Study 3: The Intersection

Lena, 25, presents with both grandiosity and auditory hallucinations.
She believes:

- She is destined for global influence
- Voices guide her decisions
- Others are either supporters or enemies

Clinicians struggle to categorize her:

- Narcissistic traits? Yes.
- Psychotic symptoms? Also, yes.

Her experience reflects the intersection of fantasy types:

- Self-constructed superiority
- Externally perceived guidance

She exists in both worlds simultaneously.

The Trap of Validation

One of the most dangerous aspects of fantasy is that it can be validated, especially in modern environments.
Social media, echo chambers, and selective relationships can reinforce distorted realities:

- Narcissistic fantasies are praised and amplified
- Delusional beliefs may go unchallenged

This external reinforcement accelerates internal entrenchment.
The individual no longer encounters reality, they encounter agreement.

Resistance to Intervention

As fantasy becomes entrenched, intervention becomes more difficult.

Why?

Because intervention threatens the system.

- Challenging narcissistic fantasy feels like an attack on identity
- Challenging schizophrenic delusion feels like denial of reality

In both cases, the individual may respond with:

- Anger
- Withdrawal
- Distrust

The very thing meant to help is perceived as harm.

The Emotional Cost of the Trap

Though fantasy provides relief, it also creates suffering:

- Relationships deteriorate
- Opportunities are lost
- Isolation increases
- Emotional regulation declines

Yet the individual may not recognize the source of the suffering.

Instead, they may believe:

- Others are the problem
- The world is unsafe
- They are misunderstood

This deepens the trap.

Fantasy as Both Refuge and Prison

At its core, fantasy serves two roles:

Refuge

- Protects from emotional pain
- Provides meaning
- Creates a sense of control

Prison

- Distorts reality
- Limits growth
- Isolates the individual
- Prevents adaptation

The same mechanism that once saved the individual now confines them.

Fantasy is not the enemy. It is a powerful human capacity, one that allows us to imagine, to create, to survive.
But when fantasy becomes the dominant lens through which reality is interpreted, it reshapes the mind itself.

In narcissism, fantasy builds a self that cannot bend.
In schizophrenia, fantasy builds a world that cannot be escaped.
In both, the individual becomes trapped, not because they chose to be, but because the mind found a way to survive and then could not let go.

And this raises the next, and most critical question:
What happens when the brain, after years of living in these constructed or distorted realities, begins to forget what reality was to begin with?

The Dimension of No Return

Fantasy, when sustained over time, does more than distort perception, it begins to reshape memory itself.

Memory is not a static recording of events. It is dynamic, constantly reconstructed, influenced by emotion, belief, and repetition. What we remember is not always what happened, but what the mind has reinforced as truth. This is where the long-term consequences of fantasy become most significant.

When an individual, whether navigating narcissism or schizophrenia—spends prolonged periods within altered realities, the brain begins to encode those realities as memory. The imagined becomes remembered. The distorted becomes familiar. And the boundary between what was lived and what was constructed begins to dissolve.

Memory as the Anchor of Reality

Reality, for most people, is grounded in memory. We know who we are because we remember where we have been. We navigate the present because we recall patterns, relationships, and outcomes. Memory is the thread that connects identity, perception, and decision-making.

But what happens when that thread is rewoven with fantasy?

In narcissism, memory is often selectively reconstructed:

- Failures are minimized or erased
- Successes are exaggerated
- Conflicts are reframed to preserve superiority

Over time, the individual does not simply reinterpret events—they begin to remember them differently. The past becomes aligned with the fantasy identity.

In schizophrenia, memory may be fragmented or distorted:

- Hallucinated experiences may be remembered as real

- Delusional beliefs become integrated into personal history
- Temporal sequencing (what happened first, what followed) becomes unclear

In both cases, memory no longer serves as a reliable anchor. It becomes an extension of the altered reality.

The Cognitive Cost of Prolonged Fantasy

The brain thrives on accuracy and adaptability. When it is consistently exposed to distortion, whether self-generated or externally perceived, it must adapt to that distortion.

This adaptation comes at a cost.

1. Impaired Reality Testing

Reality testing is the ability to distinguish between internal thoughts and external events. With prolonged fantasy immersion:

- Internal narratives override external feedback
- Contradictory information is dismissed or ignored
- The individual becomes increasingly reliant on their internal world

2. Reduced Cognitive Flexibility

Cognitive flexibility allows individuals to shift perspectives, adapt to new information, and revise beliefs.

In entrenched fantasy states:

- Beliefs become rigid
- Alternative viewpoints are rejected
- The mind resists change

3. Memory Encoding Disruption

When fantasy dominates attention, the brain prioritizes encoding those experiences over external reality.

This means:

- Real-world interactions may not be fully processed

- Imagined or distorted experiences are reinforced instead
- The distinction between "experienced" and "imagined" weakens

The Continuum Toward Cognitive Decline

This is where the central theory of this book emerges more clearly.

If narcissism and schizophrenia both involve prolonged engagement with distorted realities, and if those distortions reshape memory and cognition, then it is reasonable to consider what happens over time.

The proposal is not that these conditions directly cause dementia in a traditional clinical sense, but that they may create a parallel pathway of cognitive decline.

A progression may occur:

1. Fantasy Engagement
2. The individual uses fantasy for relief, identity, or meaning.
3. Fantasy Reinforcement
4. The brain rewards and repeats the pattern, strengthening neural pathways.
5. Reality Distortion
6. External reality becomes secondary to internal experience.
7. Memory Alteration
8. The individual begins to encode and recall distorted experiences as truth.
9. Cognitive Rigidity
10. The mind loses flexibility, resisting correction or adaptation.
11. Functional Decline
12. Relationships, decision-making, and daily functioning deteriorate.
13. The Dimension of No Return
14. The individual becomes unable to distinguish, recall, or return to baseline reality.

Understanding the "Dimension of No Return"

Case Reflection: The Long Arc

Consider two individuals over time:

Anthony, who has lived for decades within narcissistic fantasy, consistently rewriting his experiences to maintain superiority. He becomes increasingly isolated, unable to reconcile his self-image with reality. His memory of past events becomes unreliable, shaped entirely by his narrative.

Simone, who has experienced untreated schizophrenia for years. Her hallucinations and delusions have become integrated into her identity. She struggles to distinguish past events from imagined ones, and her ability to function independently declines.

Though their paths began differently, both arrive at a similar place:

- Disconnection from shared reality
- Impaired memory
- Reduced functional capacity

Both are, in different ways, living in a permanent internal dimension.

The Importance of Early Intervention

If fantasy can lead to entrenchment and cognitive decline, then early intervention becomes critical.

Intervention is not about eliminating fantasy, it is about restoring balance:

- Strengthening reality testing
- Encouraging cognitive flexibility
- Anchoring memory in shared experiences
- Creating safe spaces for confronting distortion

The goal is not to strip away the mind's protective mechanisms, but to prevent them from becoming dominant.

A Compassionate Perspective

It is essential to approach this theory with compassion.

No one chooses to become trapped in fantasy.

- The narcissistic individual is protecting a fragile self
- The schizophrenic individual is navigating overwhelming internal experiences

In both cases, the mind is attempting to survive.

Fantasy is not the enemy, it is a response.

But when that response becomes the primary way of existing, it can limit growth, connection, and ultimately, cognitive stability.

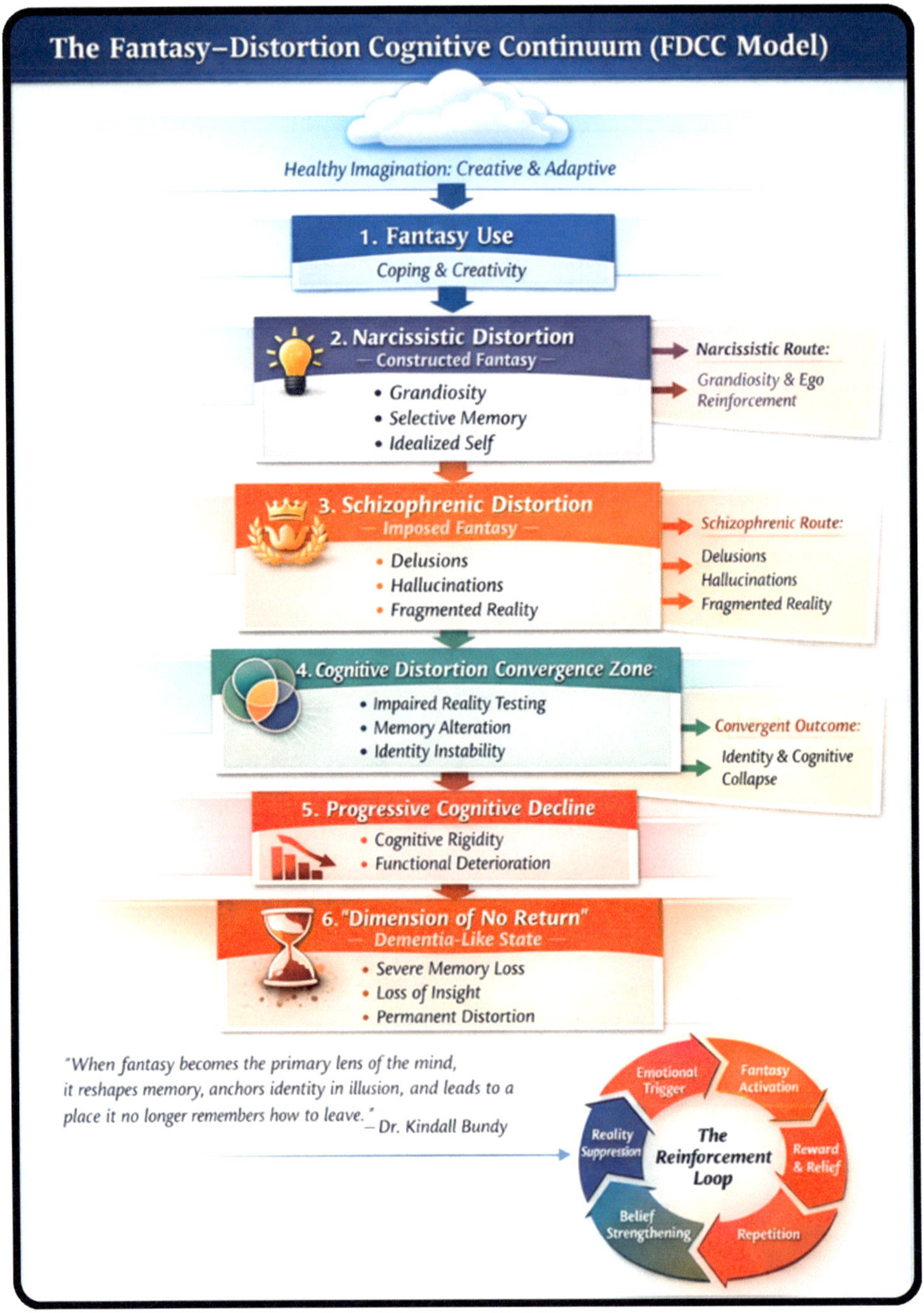
The Fantasy–Distortion Cognitive Continuum (FDCC Model)
Healthy Imagination: Creative & Adaptive
1. Fantasy Use
Coping & Creativity
2. Narcissistic Distortion
— Constructed Fantasy —
• Grandiosity
• Selective Memory
• Idealized Self
Narcissistic Route:
Grandiosity & Ego Reinforcement
3. Schizophrenic Distortion
— Imposed Fantasy —
• Delusions
• Hallucinations
• Fragmented Reality
Schizophrenic Route:
Delusions
Hallucinations
Fragmented Reality
4. Cognitive Distortion Convergence Zone
• Impaired Reality Testing
• Memory Alteration
• Identity Instability
Convergent Outcome:
Identity & Cognitive Collapse
5. Progressive Cognitive Decline
• Cognitive Rigidity
• Functional Deterioration
6. "Dimension of No Return"
— Dementia-Like State —
• Severe Memory Loss
• Loss of Insight
• Permanent Distortion
"When fantasy becomes the primary lens of the mind, it reshapes memory, anchors identity in illusion, and leads to a place it no longer remembers how to leave." – Dr. Kindall Bundy
The Reinforcement Loop
Emotional Trigger
Fantasy Activation
Reward & Relief
Repetition
Belief Strengthening
Reality Suppression

The Fantasy–Distortion Cognitive Continuum (FDCC Model)
Model Overview

The Fantasy–Distortion Cognitive Continuum (FDCC Model) presents a theoretical framework illustrating how prolonged engagement in distorted cognitive states, originating from either narcissism or schizophrenia, may converge into a shared cognitive impairment pathway. This pathway ultimately risks progression into a dementia-like state referred to as the "Dimension of No Return."

This model emphasizes fantasy as a central mechanism influencing identity formation, perception, memory, and long-term cognitive functioning.

Continuum Structure

Stage 1: Adaptive Fantasy (Healthy Functioning)

Definition:

Fantasy serves as a normal, adaptive cognitive function supporting creativity, emotional processing, and problem-solving.

Characteristics:

- Flexible thinking
- Clear distinction between reality and imagination
- Emotionally regulated responses
- Intact memory processing

Primary Brain Function:

- Default Mode Network (DMN) activation
- Balanced prefrontal cortex regulation

Stage 2: Fantasy Reinforcement (Transitional Phase)

Definition:

Fantasy becomes a repeated coping mechanism, reinforced through emotional relief and psychological reward.

Characteristics:

- Increased reliance on internal narratives
- Repetition of imagined scenarios
- Emotional dependence on fantasy for regulation
- Early distortion of perception

Key Mechanism:

- Dopamine reinforcement loop
- Beginning of cognitive preference for internal over external reality

Stage 3: Narcissistic Distortion (Constructed Fantasy Pathway)

Definition:

Fantasy is used to construct and maintain an idealized self-identity.

Characteristics:

- Grandiosity and superiority beliefs
- Selective memory reconstruction
- Reframing of failures to preserve ego
- Reduced empathy and external accountability

Cognitive Pattern:

Reality is reshaped to align with identity.

Affected Brain Regions:

- Prefrontal cortex (self-referential processing)
- Insula (emotional awareness and empathy modulation)

Stage 4: Schizophrenic Distortion (Imposed Fantasy Pathway)

Definition:

Fantasy is experienced as reality through delusions and hallucinations.

Characteristics:

- Fixed delusional beliefs
- Auditory or visual hallucinations
- Fragmented perception of reality
- Disorganized thinking

Cognitive Pattern:
Reality is replaced by internal experience.

Stage 6: Progressive Cognitive Decline
Definition:
Sustained distortion leads to measurable decline in cognitive flexibility, memory reliability, and functional behavior.
Characteristics:

- Reduced adaptability to new information
- Increasing reliance on internal narratives
- Impaired decision-making
- Social and relational deterioration

Mechanism:

- Long-term neural reinforcement of distorted pathways
- Decreased neurocognitive flexibility

Stage 7: The Dimension of No Return (Dementia-Like State)
Definition:
A chronic, entrenched state of cognitive distortion where the individual is unable to reliably return to shared reality.
Core Features:

- Persistent memory impairment
- Loss of insight
- Inability to distinguish reality from distortion
- Identity fragmentation or fixation
- Functional decline in daily living

Clinical Parallel:

- Dementia-related cognitive decline
- Chronic untreated psychosis
- Severe personality rigidity

Theoretical Position:

This state reflects not only neurological decline but also prolonged cognitive adaptation to distorted internal realities.

Central Mechanism: The Reinforcement Loop
Pathways Within the Model

Pathway A: Narcissistic Route

Adaptive Fantasy → Identity Construction → Grandiosity → Cognitive Rigidity → Convergence Zone

Pathway B: Schizophrenic Route

Perceptual Distortion → Delusions/Hallucinations → Reality Replacement → Cognitive Impairment → Convergence Zone

Pathway C: Convergent Outcome

Both pathways → Memory Alteration → Identity Instability → Cognitive Decline → Dimension of No Return

Clinical Implications

- Diagnostic frameworks should consider overlapping cognitive mechanisms rather than isolated categories
- Fantasy intensity and rigidity should be evaluated across disorders
- Early intervention should prioritize:
    - Reality anchoring strategies
    - Memory reinforcement techniques
    - Cognitive flexibility development
- Long-term untreated distortion may contribute to irreversible cognitive states

Model Summary Statement

The Fantasy–Distortion Cognitive Continuum proposes that when fantasy shifts from adaptive use to dominant cognitive function, it progressively alters perception, memory, and identity.

Across different diagnostic origins, prolonged immersion in distorted realities may lead to converging cognitive outcomes, including a dementia-like state characterized by impaired recall, reduced insight, and loss of connection to shared reality.

Closing Reflection

Fantasy is a double-edged function of the mind.
It allows us to imagine futures, process pain, and create meaning. But when it replaces reality, when it becomes the dominant framework through which we interpret the world, it begins to reshape not only perception, but memory, identity, and cognition.

In narcissism, fantasy constructs a self that cannot bend.
In schizophrenia, fantasy constructs a reality that cannot be escaped.
In both, the mind adapts to its own creation.

And if left unchallenged for too long, that adaptation may lead to a state where reality is no longer accessible, not because it disappeared, but because the mind no longer remembers how to return to it.

This is the risk.
This is the dimension.
And this is why understanding the role of fantasy is not just theoretical, it is essential.

CHAPTER 3

Dimensions of the Mind

Dimensions of the Mind

CHAPTER 3

Dimensions of the Mind

Where Reality Splits, Expands, and Reconstructs Itself

The mind is not a single, fixed space. It is not confined to one dimension of experience, one version of reality, or one stable identity. Instead, the mind operates across multiple dimensions, layers of perception, interpretation, memory, and meaning that continuously interact with one another.

For most individuals, these dimensions are integrated. Reality, imagination, memory, and identity exist in a dynamic but balanced relationship. One can imagine without losing reality. One can remember without distortion. One can adapt.

But in narcissism and schizophrenia, this balance is disrupted.

The dimensions begin to separate.

And once separated, they begin to compete.

Understanding Mental Dimensions

To understand how distortion occurs, we must first define what is meant by "dimensions of the mind."

A dimension of the mind can be understood as a layer of cognitive experience, including:

- Reality perception (what is externally verifiable)
- Internal narrative (what we tell ourselves about who we are)

- Imagination (what we create beyond reality)
- Memory (what we retain and reconstruct)
- Emotional interpretation (how we assign meaning)

In a healthy mind, these dimensions communicate fluidly:

- Reality informs memory
- Memory informs identity
- Identity shapes imagination
- Imagination enhances, but does not replace, reality

There is movement, flexibility, and integration.
But when distortion begins, these dimensions no longer align.

The Separation of Dimensions

The first shift in both narcissism and schizophrenia is not immediately visible. It does not begin with extreme behavior. It begins with subtle separation.

Reality is no longer the primary anchor.

Instead:

- Internal narrative becomes dominant (narcissism)
- Internal perception becomes dominant (schizophrenia)

This shift is critical.

Because once internal experience overrides external reality, the mind begins to reorganize itself around a new center.

Dimension One: External Reality

External reality is the shared world, the environment that can be observed, measured, and agreed upon by others.

It includes:

- Physical surroundings
- Social interactions
- Objective events

External reality is what allows individuals to function collectively. It is

the basis of communication, relationships, and decision-making.
In healthy functioning, external reality serves as the primary reference point.
But in distorted states, its authority weakens.

Dimension Two: Internal Narrative (Narcissistic Pathway)
In narcissism, the dominant dimension becomes the internal narrative.
This narrative is not random, it is carefully constructed.
It answers the question:
"Who am I?"
But instead of reflecting reality, it protects identity.
The narrative becomes:

- I am superior
- I am misunderstood
- I am deserving of more
- Others are beneath me or envious of me

This narrative is reinforced through fantasy, memory reconstruction, and selective perception.
External reality is no longer used to define identity.
Instead, it is filtered through identity.

Narrative Dominance
Once the internal narrative becomes dominant:

- Feedback is rejected if it contradicts the narrative
- Relationships are evaluated based on how well they support the narrative
- Events are interpreted to maintain the narrative

Reality becomes secondary.
The narrative becomes primary.

Dimension Three: Perceptual Distortion (Schizophrenic Pathway)

In schizophrenia, the dominant dimension is not narrative—it is perception.

The individual does not construct a story first.

They experience something first.

- A voice
- A sensation
- A feeling of being watched

These experiences are real to the individual.

The brain processes them as real.

Only afterward does the mind attempt to explain them.

Perception Before Meaning

This is a key distinction:

- Narcissism → meaning precedes perception
- Schizophrenia → perception precedes meaning

In schizophrenia, the mind asks:

"What is happening to me?"

And the answer becomes delusion.

Dimension Four: Imagination (Shared Dimension)

Imagination is the bridge between narcissism and schizophrenia.

It is the dimension where both disorders overlap.

Imagination allows:

- The narcissist to construct identity
- The schizophrenic to interpret perception

In both cases, imagination becomes expanded beyond regulation.

It no longer enhances reality.

It begins to compete with it.

When Imagination Becomes Autonomous
In healthy functioning, imagination is controlled.
You can:

- Start it
- Stop it
- Differentiate it

In distorted states, imagination becomes autonomous:

- It continues without control
- It overrides external input
- It reinforces itself

This autonomy is what allows fantasy to evolve into distortion.

Dimension Five: Memory Reconstruction

Memory is where all dimensions converge.
It is the place where:

- Reality is stored
- Narratives are reinforced
- Perceptions are integrated
- Imagination is encoded

But memory is not a recording device.
It is a reconstruction process.

And reconstruction is vulnerable to distortion.

Memory in Narcissism

In narcissism:

- Memories are edited to preserve identity
- Negative experiences are reframed
- Positive experiences are amplified

The past becomes aligned with the narrative.

Memory in Schizophrenia

In schizophrenia:

- Hallucinations may be remembered as real events
- Delusions become part of personal history
- Temporal sequencing becomes unclear

The past becomes fragmented.

Shared Outcome: Memory Instability

In both conditions:

Memory no longer reflects reality, it reflects internal experience.

This is where long-term risk emerges.

Because memory is the foundation of identity.

Dimension Six: Identity Integration

Identity is not a single thought.

It is the integration of:

- Memory
- Narrative
- Experience
- Perception

When these elements align, identity is stable.

When they do not, identity becomes unstable.

Identity in Narcissism

- Over-integrated (rigid, inflated)
- Dependent on fantasy
- Resistant to change

Identity in Schizophrenia

- Under-integrated (fragmented)
- Uncertain boundaries
- Vulnerable to distortion

Shared Instability

Though opposite in structure, both result in identity instability.
One cannot bend.
The other cannot hold.

The Dimensional Conflict

As these dimensions separate and distort, conflict emerges.

- Reality contradicts narrative
- Perception contradicts logic
- Memory contradicts experience

The mind must resolve this conflict.
But instead of restoring balance, it often chooses consistency.

Consistency Over Accuracy

The brain prioritizes:

- Internal consistency
- over
- External accuracy

This means:

- The narrative is preserved even if it is false
- The delusion is maintained even if it is illogical

The goal is not truth.
The goal is coherence.

Dimensional Dominance

At advanced stages, one dimension dominates:

- Narcissism → Narrative dominance
- Schizophrenia → Perceptual dominance

Other dimensions become subordinate.
This creates a hierarchy of cognition where:

- Reality is filtered
- Memory is altered
- Identity is fixed or fragmented

The Collapse of Integration

When dimensions no longer communicate effectively, integration collapses.

This leads to:

- Impaired reality testing
- Distorted memory
- Identity instability
- Reduced cognitive flexibility

This collapse aligns directly with your FDCC Model Convergence Zone.

Case Study: The Divided Mind

Jordan, 29, presents with both narcissistic and psychotic features.

He believes:

- He is uniquely gifted
- Others are trying to undermine him
- He receives intuitive messages guiding his decisions

His dimensions are not aligned:

- Reality contradicts his beliefs
- Perception reinforces his fears
- Memory supports his narrative

He lives in a multi-dimensional conflict, unable to reconcile the layers of his experience.

The Emergence of a New Reality

At this stage, the individual is not simply distorted—they are living in a different dimension of reality.

This dimension is:

- Internally consistent
- Emotionally reinforced
- Resistant to correction

It becomes their primary world.

The Risk of Permanence

The longer the mind operates within a distorted dimensional structure, the more it adapts to it.

Neural pathways strengthen.

Cognitive flexibility decreases.

Memory reinforces distortion.

At a certain point, returning to integrated functioning becomes increasingly difficult.

Dimensions and the "No Return" Threshold

This is where Chapter 2 and Chapter 3 converge.

The Dimension of No Return is not just cognitive decline, it is dimensional entrapment.

The individual is no longer moving between dimensions.

They are fixed within one.

- The narcissist is fixed in narrative
- The schizophrenic is fixed in perception

Reality becomes inaccessible not because it is gone, but because it is no longer the dominant dimension.

A New Way to Understand Diagnosis

This dimensional framework suggests that diagnosis should not be viewed as isolated categories, but as patterns of dimensional dominance.

Instead of asking:

"What disorder is this?"

We might ask:

"Which dimension is dominant?"

"How are the dimensions interacting?"

"Where has integration broken down?"

This shift allows for more nuanced understanding—and more targeted intervention.

Restoring Dimensional Balance

If distortion is the result of dimensional imbalance, then treatment must focus on re-integration.

This includes:

- Strengthening reality testing
- Reconstructing accurate memory
- Encouraging flexible thinking
- Supporting identity development

The goal is not to eliminate imagination, narrative, or perception.

The goal is to restore communication between dimensions.

Closing Reflection

The mind is not broken in these conditions, it is reorganized.

It has shifted from integration to separation, from balance to dominance, from flexibility to rigidity.

Narcissism and schizophrenia, though different in origin, reveal the same underlying truth:

When one dimension of the mind becomes dominant, the others begin to fade. At the same time, when enough dimensions fade, the individual is left with a reality that is internally consistent, but externally disconnected.

Understanding these dimensions is not just theoretical.

It is essential. Because within this understanding lies the possibility of prevention, intervention, and perhaps most importantly,retun .

CHAPTER 4

Neurological Pathways

Neurological Pathways

CHAPTER 4

Neurological Pathways
Where Structure, Chemistry, and Perception Converge
The mind does not distort in isolation.

Every thought, perception, memory, and identity formation is rooted in neural activity, patterns of firing neurons, chemical signaling, and structural connectivity across brain regions. To understand the progression from adaptive fantasy to cognitive distortion, we must move beyond psychological theory and into the biological systems that sustain it.

Schizophrenia and narcissism, though often discussed as distinct conditions, share a critical intersection: both involve disruptions in neural pathways responsible for self-perception, emotional regulation, and memory integration.

This chapter explores those pathways.

The Brain as a Predictive Organ

Before examining specific structures, it is essential to understand a foundational principle: the brain is not a passive receiver of reality, it is a predictive organ.

It continuously:

- Anticipates incoming sensory information
- Interprets experiences based on prior memory
- Constructs meaning before full awareness

This process, often described as predictive coding, allows for efficient functioning. However, when prediction overrides reality, distortion begins.

In both schizophrenia and narcissism:

- The brain prioritizes internal models over external input
- Perception becomes shaped by expectation
- Reality becomes filtered, altered, or replaced

Schizophrenia: Disruption Across Core Neural Systems

Schizophrenia is not localized to a single brain region. It is a disorder of network dysfunction, particularly involving the prefrontal cortex, hippocampus, and amygdala.

The Prefrontal Cortex: Executive Breakdown

The prefrontal cortex (PFC) is responsible for:

- Decision-making
- Reality testing
- Impulse control
- Cognitive flexibility

In schizophrenia, the PFC often shows hypoactivity, meaning reduced functioning.

This results in:

- Impaired judgment
- Difficulty distinguishing internal thoughts from external reality
- Reduced ability to correct false beliefs

Impact on Reality Testing

Reality testing requires the ability to:

- Compare internal thoughts with external evidence
- Adjust beliefs when contradictions arise

When the PFC is compromised:

- Delusions persist despite contradictory evidence
- Hallucinations are interpreted as real
- Logical reasoning weakens

The mind loses its ability to "check itself."

The Hippocampus: Memory and Context Distortion

The hippocampus plays a central role in:

- Memory formation
- Contextual processing
- Distinguishing past from present

In schizophrenia, the hippocampus is often overactive and structurally altered.

Consequences of Hippocampal Dysfunction

- Memories may be misattributed or distorted
- Internal experiences may feel externally generated
- Context becomes fragmented

This contributes directly to:

- Delusions ("This happened to me")
- Hallucinations ("I hear something real")

The brain struggles to anchor experiences in time and space.

The Amygdala: Emotional Misattribution

The amygdala regulates:

- Emotional salience
- Fear processing
- Threat detection

In schizophrenia, amygdala activity is often dysregulated.

Hyper-Salience and Threat Perception

Neutral stimuli may be interpreted as:

- Threatening
- Significant
- Personally relevant

This leads to:

- Paranoia
- Suspicion
- Emotional intensity attached to false beliefs

The brain assigns importance where none exists.

The Schizophrenic Circuit

Together, these regions create a dysfunctional loop:

1. Hippocampus generates distorted memory/context
2. Amygdala assigns emotional significance
3. Prefrontal cortex fails to regulate or correct

The result is a self-reinforcing system of distortion.

Narcissism: A Different Pathway, A Similar Outcome

While schizophrenia is marked by perceptual disruption, narcissism is rooted in self-processing and emotional regulation networks.

The primary regions involved include:

- Prefrontal cortex
- Insula
- Limbic system

The Prefrontal Cortex: Strategic Control

Unlike schizophrenia, narcissism often involves selective PFC activation.

The PFC is used to:

- Construct self-enhancing narratives
- Suppress contradictory information
- Maintain control in social interactions

Cognitive Control Without Flexibility

The narcissistic brain does not lack control, it lacks flexibility.

- Information is filtered to preserve identity
- Criticism is dismissed or reframed
- Decision-making is biased toward self-preservation

The PFC becomes a tool for identity defense.

The Insula: Impaired Emotional Awareness

The insula is critical for:

- Interoception (awareness of internal states)
- Empathy
- Emotional integration

Research suggests that individuals with narcissistic traits often show reduced insula activation.

Consequences of Insular Dysfunction

- Limited empathy
- Difficulty recognizing others' emotional states
- Reduced connection between emotional experience and behavior

This contributes to:

- Emotional detachment
- Exploitative behavior
- Lack of accountability

The Limbic System: Dysregulated Emotion

The limbic system governs:

- Emotional response
- Reward processing
- Attachment

In narcissism, limbic functioning is often imbalanced.

Emotional Extremes

- Hypersensitivity to criticism
- Heightened reward response to admiration
- Rapid shifts between superiority and vulnerability

This creates emotional instability beneath a controlled exterior.

Overlap: Where the Pathways Meet

Despite their differences, schizophrenia and narcissism share key neurological overlaps.

These overlaps are critical to your FDCC model.

1. The Prefrontal Cortex: Impaired Regulation

- Schizophrenia → underactive PFC (loss of control)
- Narcissism → selectively active PFC (rigid control)

In both cases:

Reality testing is compromised.

2. Memory Circuits: Distorted Reconstruction

Both conditions involve dysfunction in:

- Hippocampal processing
- Memory integration

Resulting in:

- Altered perception of past events
- Reinforcement of distorted identity

3. Self-Perception Networks

Both conditions disrupt how the brain constructs the "self."

This involves:

- Default Mode Network (DMN)
- Medial prefrontal cortex
- Posterior cingulate cortex

Distorted Self-Representation

- Narcissism → inflated, rigid self
- Schizophrenia → fragmented, unstable self

Both reflect disrupted self-processing systems.

4. Salience Network Dysfunction

The salience network determines:

"What matters?"

In both conditions:

- Irrelevant information may feel important
- Internal thoughts may feel external
- Emotional responses may not match reality

The Role of Neurochemistry

Neurotransmitters further shape these pathways.

Dopamine

Dopamine is central to:

- Reward
- Motivation
- Salience detection

In Schizophrenia

- Excess dopamine activity
- Leads to hallucinations and delusions
- Assigns meaning to irrelevant stimuli

Glutamate

Glutamate regulates:

- Learning
- Memory
- Neural communication

Dysregulation contributes to:

- Cognitive fragmentation
- Impaired integration

Neuroplasticity and Reinforcement

The brain adapts to repeated patterns.

- Repeated fantasy strengthens imagination pathways
- Repeated distortion strengthens belief systems
- Repeated emotional reinforcement solidifies identity

This is the neurological foundation of your Reinforcement Loop.

"Neurons That Fire Together, Wire Together"

Over time:

- Distorted thinking becomes automatic
- Alternative interpretations weaken
- Cognitive rigidity increases

The brain becomes trained in distortion.

Case Study: Neurological Convergence

Danielle, 35, presents with:

- Grandiose self-beliefs
- Episodes of paranoia
- Emotional dysregulation

Neurologically:

- Heightened limbic reactivity
- Reduced insula integration
- Impaired prefrontal flexibility

Her presentation reflects overlap between narcissistic and psychotic pathways.
She does not fit neatly into one diagnosis.
Instead, she exists within a continuum of neural dysfunction.

From Pathways to Collapse

As dysfunction progresses:

- Neural communication weakens
- Integration fails
- Compensation strategies break down

This leads to:

- Identity instability
- Cognitive rigidity
- Emotional dysregulation

Eventually, the brain can no longer maintain coherence.

The Neurological Basis of the "Dimension of No Return"

Your FDCC model's final stage is not just psychological, it is neurological.
At this stage:

- Neural pathways are deeply reinforced
- Plasticity is reduced
- Distortion becomes the dominant mode of functioning

The brain is no longer flexible.
It is fixed.

Implications for Treatment

Understanding these pathways changes how we approach intervention.

1. Early Intervention Matters

Neural pathways are more flexible early on.
Addressing:

- Fantasy reliance
- Cognitive distortion
- Emotional dysregulation

can prevent long-term entrenchment.

2. Targeting Integration

Treatment must focus on:

- Strengthening prefrontal regulation
- Reconnecting emotional awareness (insula)
- Stabilizing memory processing (hippocampus)

3. Beyond Diagnosis

Rather than treating labels, we must treat:

- Pathways
- Patterns
- Networks

Figure 1. Neural Pathways in the Fantasy–Distortion Cognitive Continuum (FDCC Model)

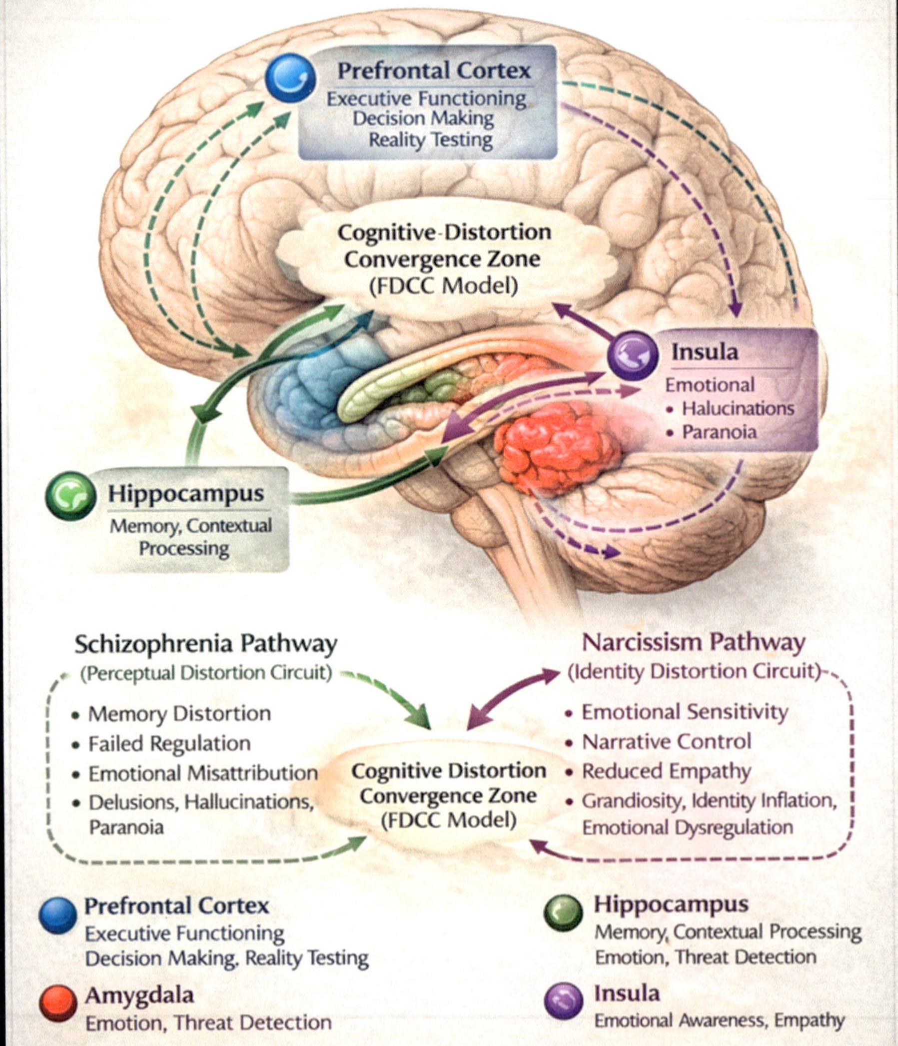

This diagram illustrates the primary brain regions implicated in the development of cognitive distortion. Disrupted communication between these areas contrributes to impaired reality testing, distorted memory reconstruction, and altered self-perception.

Figure 1. Neural Pathways in the Fantasy–Distortion Cognitive Continuum (FDCC Model).

This diagram illustrates the primary brain regions implicated in the development of cognitive distortion across narcissistic and schizophrenic pathways. The prefrontal cortex (PFC) is associated with executive functioning, decision-making, and reality testing. The hippocampus is responsible for memory formation and contextual processing, while the amygdala governs emotional salience and threat detection. The insula contributes to emotional awareness, empathy, and interoceptive processing. Dysregulation across these regions contributes to impaired reality testing, distorted memory reconstruction, and altered self-perception, forming the neurological basis of the FDCC Model.

Closing Reflection

The brain does not fail randomly.
It adapts.
It compensates.
It reorganizes.
Schizophrenia and narcissism reveal two different adaptations to internal and external stress, one driven by perception, the other by identity. Yet both converge in the same place:

A mind shaped more by internal construction than external reality.
Understanding these neurological pathways is not simply about identifying dysfunction. It is about recognizing how the brain learns, how it protects itself, and how, over time, those protections can become prisons.
And once the pathways are deeply embedded, the question is no longer:
"What is real?"
But rather:
"What has the brain learned to believe is real, and can it be taught otherwise?"

CHAPTER 5

The Spectrum Toward Dementia

The Spectrum Toward Dementia

CHAPTER 5

The Spectrum Toward Dementia

Introduction: When the Mind Can No Longer Return

There exists a threshold within the human mind, a point where distortion, if left unchallenged and untreated, no longer remains flexible. It becomes fixed. What once functioned as a psychological defense, a coping mechanism, or even a fragmented perception of reality begins to solidify into permanence. This is where the continuum explored throughout this book reaches its most critical stage, the potential progression toward dementia.

Within the framework of the Fantasy–Distortion Cognitive Continuum (FDCC Model), dementia is conceptualized not only as a neurological condition but as the far end of prolonged cognitive disruption. It represents a "dimension of no return," where memory, identity, and reality-testing capacities deteriorate to a point where reconstruction becomes increasingly difficult.

This chapter does not claim that narcissism or schizophrenia directly causes dementia in a traditional medical sense. Instead, it presents a theory: that chronic engagement in distorted cognitive states—particularly those driven by unregulated fantasy, may place sustained strain on neural systems responsible for memory, perception, and identity, potentially accelerating cognitive decline or mimicking dementia-like presentations.

Defining Dementia: A Clinical and Cognitive Perspective

Dementia is not a single disease but a broad term used to describe a decline in cognitive functioning severe enough to interfere with daily life. It primarily affects:

- Memory
- Reasoning and judgment
- Language and communication
- Attention and executive functioning
- Emotional regulation

The most commonly recognized forms include Alzheimer's disease, vascular dementia, and frontotemporal dementia. At its core, dementia involves progressive neurodegeneration, particularly within the hippocampus, prefrontal cortex, and temporal lobes, regions already implicated in both schizophrenia and narcissistic pathology.

However, beyond the biological definition lies a cognitive reality: dementia represents a breakdown in the brain's ability to organize, retrieve, and accurately interpret reality over time.

This is where the FDCC model becomes relevant.

The FDCC Continuum and Cognitive Fatigue

The FDCC model proposes that the mind exists on a continuum between:

- Reality Anchoring (stable perception, flexible thinking)
- Fantasy Engagement (adaptive imagination, coping)
- Distorted Reality (rigid belief systems, impaired perception)
- Cognitive Entrapment (inability to differentiate internal vs. external reality)
- Cognitive Degradation (memory and identity breakdown)

Dementia emerges conceptually at the far end of this continuum, not necessarily as a direct cause of earlier stages, but as a potential outcome when cognitive systems are repeatedly overtaxed.

Cognitive Load and Neural Exhaustion

The brain is not designed to continuously reconcile conflicting realities. When an individual persistently operates within distorted frameworks:

- The prefrontal cortex becomes overburdened attempting to maintain coherence
- The hippocampus struggles to encode accurate memories versus imagined ones
- The amygdala remains in a heightened state of emotional activation

Over time, this creates what can be described as cognitive fatigue, a state in which the brain's regulatory systems weaken.

Narcissism and the Erosion of Reality-Based Memory

Narcissism, particularly in its pathological form, is deeply rooted in constructed identity narratives. These narratives are often:

- Idealized
- Selectively remembered
- Emotionally reinforced
- Resistant to contradiction

Memory Reconstruction vs. Memory Distortion

The narcissistic mind does not simply recall memories, it reconstructs them in alignment with identity preservation. Over time, this repeated reconstruction can lead to:

- Inconsistent autobiographical memory
- Emotional rewriting of past events
- Difficulty distinguishing between what happened and what was needed psychologically

This process places significant strain on the hippocampus, which is responsible for memory consolidation. When memory becomes a tool for self-protection rather than accurate recall, the brain begins to prioritize coherence over truth.

Schizophrenia and the Breakdown of Reality Processing

Schizophrenia presents a different but equally taxing pathway.

Rather than reconstructing reality, the schizophrenic mind often experiences:

- Delusions (fixed false beliefs)
- Hallucinations (perceptions without external stimuli)
- Disorganized thinking

The Collapse of Reality Testing

The prefrontal cortex, responsible for evaluating what is real versus imagined, becomes impaired. Simultaneously:

- The hippocampus may encode distorted experiences as real memories
- The amygdala amplifies emotional responses to these distortions

This creates a loop where:

Distorted perception → Emotional reinforcement → Memory encoding → Reinforced belief

Over time, this loop can lead to deep entrenchment, where the individual no longer questions their internal reality.

Fantasy as a Shared Mechanism of Cognitive Strain

One of the central arguments of this book is that fantasy is not inherently harmful. It is, in fact, essential for creativity, planning, and emotional processing.

However, when fantasy becomes:

- Chronic
- Unregulated
- Detached from reality testing

It shifts from adaptive to maladaptive.

The Brain's Burden

Maintaining a fantasy-based internal world requires:

- Continuous cognitive energy

- Emotional investment
- Neural coordination across multiple brain regions

When this becomes the dominant mode of processing, the brain is forced to operate in a state of ongoing simulation, rather than grounded reality.

This is not sustainable indefinitely.

The Convergence Point: When Distortion Becomes Degeneration

Within the FDCC model, both narcissism and schizophrenia converge at a critical point:

The Cognitive Distortion Convergence Zone

At this stage:

- Reality is no longer flexible
- Memory is no longer reliable
- Identity becomes unstable or overly rigid

The brain begins to lose its ability to:

- Correct errors
- Integrate new information
- Adapt to changing environments

This is where the risk of long-term cognitive impairment increases.

The Theory: Prolonged Distortion and the Pathway to Dementia

The central theory proposed in this chapter is as follows:

When the brain remains in a prolonged state of cognitive distortion, whether through narcissistic identity reinforcement or schizophrenic perceptual disruption, it may contribute to long-term strain on neural systems responsible for memory, reality testing, and identity integration, potentially increasing vulnerability to dementia-like cognitive decline.

Key Mechanisms of Risk

- Chronic Stress on Neural Circuits

Persistent activation of emotional and cognitive distortion pathways weakens regulatory systems.

- Memory Encoding Disruption

The hippocampus struggles to differentiate between real and constructed experiences.

- Reduced Neuroplasticity

Rigid belief systems limit the brain's ability to adapt and reorganize.

- Emotional Dysregulation

The amygdala remains overactive, impairing cognitive clarity.

- Identity Fragmentation or Rigidity

The self becomes either unstable or excessively fixed, both of which reduce cognitive flexibility.

Case Illustration (Composite Example)

Consider two individuals over a 20-year span:

Case A: Narcissistic Pattern

- Rewrites personal history to maintain superiority
- Avoids contradictory feedback
- Reinforces fantasy-based identity

Outcome: Increasing confusion when confronted with reality, difficulty recalling accurate events, emotional instability.

Case B: Schizophrenic Pattern

- Experiences persistent delusions
- Interprets internal stimuli as external
- Encodes distorted experiences as memory

Outcome: Deepened detachment from shared reality, impaired functioning, memory inconsistencies.

Shared Endpoint

Both individuals begin to exhibit:

- Memory lapses
- Disorganized thinking
- Reduced ability to function independently

While their origins differ, their cognitive outcomes begin to resemble one another.

Dementia as a "Dimension of No Return"

In the context of the FDCC model, dementia is conceptualized as:

A state in which the brain can no longer effectively reconstruct, correct, or stabilize reality due to sustained cognitive and neurological degradation.

At this stage:

- Intervention becomes more difficult
- Identity may dissolve or become unrecognizable
- Memory loss becomes progressive

This is not simply forgetting, it is losing the ability to anchor oneself in reality.

Hope, Intervention, and Prevention

While this chapter explores a serious trajectory, it is equally important to emphasize:

The Brain Is Adaptable

Early intervention can:

- Restore reality testing
- Improve emotional regulation
- Strengthen memory pathways

Protective Factors Include:

- Therapeutic engagement
- Reality-based grounding techniques
- Cognitive behavioral interventions

- Social connection and accountability
- Medical and psychiatric support

The continuum is not fixed. Movement is possible, both toward distortion and back toward clarity.

Closing Reflection

The human mind is powerful, imaginative, and deeply complex. It is capable of constructing entire worlds, worlds that can comfort, protect, and inspire. But when those worlds replace reality, when they become the dominant lens through which life is experienced, the cost can be profound.

Narcissism and schizophrenia, though distinct, reveal a shared truth: The mind, when left in distortion for too long, begins to forget how to return.

And in that forgetting, we encounter the edge of something irreversible.

CHAPTER 6

The Continuum Theory

The Continuum Theory

CHAPTER 6

The Continuum Theory
Introduction: One Mind, Multiple Expressions
For decades, mental health diagnoses have been treated as distinct categories, separate conditions with separate causes, symptoms, and treatments. Narcissistic Personality Disorder and Schizophrenia are often viewed as fundamentally different: one rooted in personality and identity, the other in perception and psychosis.

Yet, when we move beyond diagnostic labels and examine the underlying cognitive processes, a different picture begins to emerge. This chapter introduces a unifying framework:
Narcissism, schizophrenia, and dementia are not isolated conditions, but points along a single cognitive continuum shaped by the brain's relationship with reality, fantasy, and identity.

Within the Fantasy–Distortion Cognitive Continuum (FDCC Model), these conditions represent progressive shifts in how the mind constructs, maintains, and ultimately loses its connection to reality.

The FDCC Continuum: A Unified Model of Cognitive Distortion

The FDCC Continuum proposes that the human mind operates along a spectrum defined by its ability to:

- Accurately perceive reality
- Integrate memory
- Maintain a stable identity
- Regulate emotional experiences

When these systems function optimally, individuals remain grounded, adaptable, and capable of self-correction.

However, when these systems become distorted, the mind begins to move along a continuum:

Stage 1: Reality Anchoring (Healthy Functioning)

- Accurate perception of self and environment
- Flexible thinking and emotional regulation
- Reliable memory integration
- Capacity for reflection and correction

Stage 2: Adaptive Fantasy (Normal Imagination)

- Daydreaming, creativity, and goal visualization
- Temporary escape without loss of reality testing
- Supports emotional processing and innovation

Stage 3: Narcissistic Distortion (Identity-Based Fantasy)

- Self-enhancing narratives become rigid
- Memory begins to align with identity preservation
- Reduced empathy and selective perception
- Reality is filtered, not lost

Key Feature: Reality is still present but reshaped to protect identity.

Stage 4: Schizophrenic Distortion (Perceptual Breakdown)

- Reality testing becomes impaired
- Delusions and hallucinations emerge

- Internal experiences are perceived as external
- Memory encoding becomes unreliable

Key Feature: Reality is no longer filtered, it is fragmented.

Stage 5: Cognitive Entrapment (Convergence Zone)

- Distortion becomes fixed and resistant to correction
- Identity and perception begin to collapse or rigidify
- Neural systems struggle to differentiate truth from fabrication

Key Feature: The mind becomes trapped within its own constructed reality.

Stage 6: Dementia (Cognitive Degradation)

- Memory systems deteriorate
- Identity becomes unstable or dissolves
- Reality anchoring is significantly impaired or lost

Key Feature: The mind can no longer reconstruct or return to reality.

Narcissism ↔ Schizophrenia ↔ Dementia: One Continuum

At first glance, narcissism and schizophrenia appear fundamentally different. However, within the FDCC model, they represent different entry points into the same continuum.

Narcissism: Distortion Begins with Identity

- The self is inflated or protected through fantasy
- Reality is reshaped to maintain internal coherence
- Memory becomes selective

Schizophrenia: Distortion Begins with Perception

- External reality is misinterpreted
- Internal experiences override sensory input
- Memory becomes disorganized

The Convergence

Despite their differences, both pathways lead to:

- Impaired reality testing
- Distorted memory encoding
- Emotional dysregulation

- Reduced cognitive flexibility

This convergence forms the Cognitive Distortion Convergence Zone, where distinctions between the two begin to blur.

Dementia: The Dimension of No Return

Within this continuum, dementia represents a critical threshold:
A state in which the brain loses its ability to correct, reconstruct, or stabilize reality due to sustained cognitive and neurological degradation.

Why "No Return"?

Dementia is characterized by:

- Progressive neuronal loss
- Reduced neuroplasticity
- Breakdown of memory consolidation systems

At this stage:

- The brain cannot reliably distinguish past from present
- Identity becomes fragmented or absent
- Reality is no longer accessible in a consistent way

Unlike earlier stages of the continuum, where intervention can restore function, dementia represents a point where recovery becomes significantly limited.

The Core Theory: Distorted Reality and Neural Change

At the center of this chapter is the defining theory of the FDCC model:
Long-term immersion in distorted cognitive realities—whether through identity-based fantasy (narcissism) or perceptual distortion (schizophrenia) can lead to sustained strain on neural systems, potentially contributing to permanent changes in brain function.

Mechanisms of Neural Change

1. Chronic Activation of Distortion Pathways

Repeated engagement in distorted thinking strengthens neural circuits associated with:

- Fantasy reinforcement
- Emotional reactivity
- Narrative control

This follows the principle:
"Neurons that fire together wire together."

2. Impaired Reality Testing (Prefrontal Cortex Dysfunction)

The prefrontal cortex is responsible for:

- Decision-making
- Self-reflection
- Reality evaluation

When consistently overridden:

- Reality testing weakens
- Cognitive flexibility decreases

3. Memory Encoding Disruption (Hippocampal Strain)

The hippocampus encodes experiences into memory.
In distorted states:

- False or altered experiences are encoded as real
- Memory becomes unreliable

Over time:

- The brain loses the ability to distinguish accurate recall from constructed narrative

4. Emotional Overactivation (Amygdala Dysregulation)

The amygdala amplifies emotional responses.
In both narcissism and schizophrenia:

- Emotional intensity reinforces distorted beliefs
- Fear, shame, or grandiosity becomes neurologically embedded

The Role of Time: Duration Matters

One of the most critical components of this theory is duration.

Short-term distortion:

- May be reversible
- Allows for intervention

Long-term distortion:

- Reinforces maladaptive neural pathways
- Reduces neuroplasticity
- Increases risk of cognitive decline

It is not only the presence of distortion, but the length of time one remains within it, that determines long-term impact.

Identity, Memory, and the Fragility of Reality

At its core, this continuum is about three interconnected systems:

1. Identity

- Who am I?

2. Memory

- What have I experienced?

3. Reality

- What is true?

When these systems align, the mind is stable.

When they diverge:

- Identity becomes defensive or fragmented
- Memory becomes distorted
- Reality becomes negotiable

When they collapse:

- The individual loses the ability to anchor themselves in the world

Clinical and Theoretical Implications

This continuum challenges traditional diagnostic boundaries and suggests:

- The need for early intervention across disorders
- A focus on cognitive processes rather than labels

- Recognition of shared neurological vulnerabilities

It also raises critical questions:

- Could some cases of misdiagnosis stem from observing different points on the same continuum?
- Are we treating symptoms without addressing underlying cognitive distortion patterns?
- How can we intervene before distortion becomes permanent?

Hope Within the Continuum

While this chapter explores progression, it also reinforces an essential truth:

The brain is not fixed, it is adaptive.

Before reaching the later stages:

- Neural pathways can be redirected
- Reality testing can be strengthened
- Identity can be reconstructed in healthy ways

Intervention is most effective when:

- Distortion is recognized early
- Support systems are engaged
- Cognitive flexibility is restored

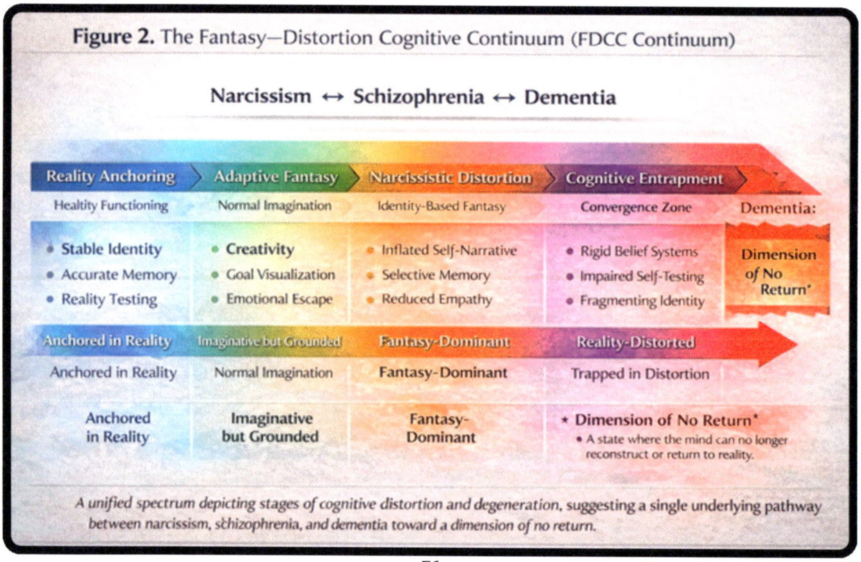

Figure 2. The Fantasy—Distortion Cognitive Continuum (FDCC Continuum)

A unified spectrum depicting stages of cognitive distortion and degeneration, suggesting a single underlying pathway between narcissism, schizophrenia, and dementia toward a dimension of no return.

Closing Reflection: The Mind's Greatest Strength and Vulnerability

The human mind is capable of extraordinary things. It can imagine, create, protect, and transform. But it can also deceive, distort, and entrap itself.

Narcissism, schizophrenia, and dementia, when viewed through the FDCC lens are not isolated disorders. They are reflections of a deeper truth:

The mind becomes what it repeatedly believes.

And when belief drifts too far from reality for too long, the path back becomes harder to find.

CHAPTER 7

Implications for Diagnosis and Treatment

Implications for Diagnosis and Treatment

CHAPTER 7

Correcting the Course Before the Mind Drifts Too Far

Introduction: The Cost of Getting It Wrong

Diagnosis is not simply a label; it is a direction. It determines treatment, shapes perception, and ultimately influences outcomes. Within the framework of the Fantasy Distortion Cognitive Continuum (FDCC), misdiagnosis is not a minor clinical error; it is a pivotal turning point that can accelerate a person's movement along the continuum from distorted perception to irreversible cognitive decline.

When narcissism is mistaken for schizophrenia, or schizophrenia is misunderstood as narcissistic personality traits, the consequences are profound. Treatment becomes misaligned. Interventions miss their target. Most critically, the individual's internal experience remains unaddressed, allowing fantasy, distortion, and cognitive fragmentation to deepen.

This chapter explores the real-world implications of misdiagnosis, the urgency of early intervention, and the essential role of anchoring individuals back to reality through structured therapeutic, cognitive, and neurological approaches.

Section I: The Dangers of Misdiagnosis

1. Misdiagnosis as a Catalyst for Cognitive Decline

Within the FDCC model, misdiagnosis acts as a reinforcement mechanism. Instead of interrupting maladaptive cognitive patterns, it validates them, either directly or indirectly.

- A person with narcissistic pathology may be misdiagnosed with a psychotic disorder, leading clinicians to focus solely on hallucinations or delusions while overlooking ego defense mechanisms, identity fragility, and emotional dysregulation.
- Conversely, an individual with schizophrenia may be labeled as narcissistic, particularly when presenting with guardedness, detachment, or perceived grandiosity, causing providers to miss neurochemical and perceptual disturbances requiring medical treatment.

In both cases, the individual becomes trapped in a cycle where:

- Symptoms are misunderstood
- Interventions are ineffective
- Distorted thinking is unintentionally reinforced

This creates a dangerous trajectory, one that pushes the individual further along the continuum toward cognitive rigidity and eventual deterioration.

2. Behavioral Overlap: Where Clinicians Get Confused

Misdiagnosis often occurs because behavioral presentations overlap in ways that appear deceptively similar:

Observed Behavior	Narcissism Interpretation	Schizophrenia Interpretation
Grandiose beliefs	Inflated self-importance	Delusional thinking
Emotional detachment	Lack of empathy	Negative symptoms (flat affect)
Suspicion of others	Paranoia rooted in ego defense	Paranoid delusions
Distorted narratives	Self-enhancing storytelling	Reality distortion

Without a deep assessment of:

- Insight levels
- Cognitive organization
- Reality testing capacity
- Neurological functioning

...it becomes easy to mistake defensive fantasy for psychosis or psychosis for personality structure.

3. The Emotional Toll of Being Misunderstood

Beyond clinical implications, misdiagnosis has a profound human cost.

Individuals may experience:

- Chronic invalidation ("That's not what I'm feeling.")
- Increased isolation
- Distrust in providers
- Escalation of symptoms due to lack of appropriate care

For families and caregivers, the confusion can be equally damaging. They may:

- Respond incorrectly to behaviors
- Reinforce maladaptive patterns unknowingly
- Experience burnout from ineffective support strategies

Misdiagnosis does not just delay healing, it reshapes the entire trajectory of a person's life.

Section II: Why Early Intervention Matters

1. The Window of Cognitive Plasticity

The brain is not static. Especially in early stages of mental health conditions, it retains a significant degree of plasticity, the ability to reorganize, adapt, and recover.

Within the FDCC framework:

- Early-stage narcissistic distortion can be restructured
- Early psychotic symptoms can be stabilized
- Cognitive pathways can be redirected before they solidify

However, as distortion becomes chronic:

- Neural pathways strengthen maladaptive patterns
- Reality testing weakens
- Memory and identity begin to fragment

This progression is what ultimately leads toward the "dimension of no return", a state resembling dementia, where cognitive recovery becomes increasingly limited.

2. Intervening Before Identity Collapse

One of the most critical intervention points is before identity collapse occurs.

In narcissism:

- The false self begins to dominate
- Authentic identity becomes inaccessible

In schizophrenia:

- The sense of self becomes fragmented
- Internal and external realities blur

Early intervention helps:

- Preserve identity coherence
- Strengthen self-awareness
- Prevent full immersion into distorted realities

3. The Role of Screening and Differential Diagnosis

Accurate diagnosis requires a multi-layered approach:

- Psychological assessment
- Neurocognitive testing
- Behavioral observation over time
- Medical and neurological evaluation

Key differentiators include:

- Presence of hallucinations (more aligned with schizophrenia)
- Degree of insight (often higher in narcissism, though limited)
- Emotional reactivity vs. emotional blunting
- Consistency vs. fragmentation of identity

Without a deep assessment of:

- Insight levels
- Cognitive organization
- Reality testing capacity
- Neurological functioning

...it becomes easy to mistake defensive fantasy for psychosis or psychosis for personality structure.

3. The Emotional Toll of Being Misunderstood

Beyond clinical implications, misdiagnosis has a profound human cost.

Individuals may experience:

- Chronic invalidation ("That's not what I'm feeling.")
- Increased isolation
- Distrust in providers
- Escalation of symptoms due to lack of appropriate care

For families and caregivers, the confusion can be equally damaging. They may:

- Respond incorrectly to behaviors
- Reinforce maladaptive patterns unknowingly
- Experience burnout from ineffective support strategies

Misdiagnosis does not just delay healing, it reshapes the entire trajectory of a person's life.

Section II: Why Early Intervention Matters

1. The Window of Cognitive Plasticity

The brain is not static. Especially in early stages of mental health conditions, it retains a significant degree of plasticity—the ability to reorganize, adapt, and recover.

Within the FDCC framework:

- Early-stage narcissistic distortion can be restructured
- Early psychotic symptoms can be stabilized
- Cognitive pathways can be redirected before they solidify

Early and accurate diagnosis allows for targeted intervention, reducing long-term risk.

Section III: Anchoring Patients in Reality

At the core of treatment within the FDCC model is a singular goal:
To anchor the individual back to reality before distortion becomes permanent.
This requires a combination of psychological, cognitive, and neurological strategies.

1. Cognitive Behavioral Therapy (CBT): Rebuilding Thought Structures

CBT serves as a foundational tool for addressing distorted thinking patterns.

For Narcissism:

- Challenging grandiose beliefs
- Increasing accountability
- Developing empathy and perspective-taking

For Schizophrenia:

- Reality testing exercises
- Identifying cognitive distortions
- Managing delusional thought patterns

CBT helps individuals:

- Recognize the difference between perception and reality
- Develop tools to question their own thinking
- Reduce reliance on fantasy as a coping mechanism

2. Memory Exercises: Strengthening Cognitive Anchors

Memory plays a critical role in maintaining a stable sense of reality.
When memory weakens:

- Fantasy fills the gaps
- Distorted narratives become "truth"

Memory-focused interventions include:

- Daily recall exercises
- Journaling to track reality-based events

- Structured routines that reinforce temporal awareness
- Cognitive training programs targeting executive functioning

These exercises help ground individuals in:

- Time
- Place
- Personal identity

3. Neurological Screenings: Identifying Underlying Changes

Because the FDCC model links psychological distortion to potential neurological decline, regular screenings are essential.

These may include:

- Brain imaging (MRI, CT scans when indicated)
- Cognitive assessments (MMSE, MoCA)
- Neuropsychological evaluations

Early detection of:

- Memory impairment
- Executive dysfunction
- Structural brain changes

...allows for interventions that may slow or alter progression toward dementia.

4. Medication and Integrated Care

For individuals with schizophrenia or significant cognitive disturbance:

- Antipsychotic medications may stabilize perception
- Mood stabilizers may reduce emotional volatility
- Integrated care models combine therapy, medication, and social support

For narcissistic pathology:

- Medication is not primary but may support co-occurring conditions (e.g., depression, anxiety)

The key is alignment, ensuring treatment matches the underlying condition.

5. Social and Environmental Anchoring

Reality is not just internal, it is reinforced externally.

Support systems play a critical role in:

- Providing consistent feedback
- Reinforcing grounded perspectives
- Interrupting distorted narratives

Effective strategies include:

- Structured environments
- Accountability partnerships
- Psychoeducation for families

Without external anchors, individuals are more likely to drift deeper into internal distortions.

Section IV: Preventing the Continuum from Progressing

The ultimate goal of diagnosis and treatment is not just symptom reduction, it is prevention of progression along the FDCC continuum.

Key Prevention Strategies:

- Early identification of distorted thinking
- Accurate differential diagnosis
- Consistent therapeutic engagement
- Cognitive and memory reinforcement
- Neurological monitoring

Closing Reflection: Restoring Clarity Before It Is Lost

The FDCC model challenges us to rethink how we understand and treat mental health conditions. It asks us to look beyond labels and into the underlying mechanisms of distortion, fantasy, and cognitive decline. Misdiagnosis is not just an error; it is a missed opportunity to intervene.

Early intervention is not just helpful, it is essential. Anchoring individuals in reality is not just a therapeutic goal; it is a lifeline. Because once the mind drifts too far, once memory begins to fade, once identity becomes untethered, the path back becomes increasingly difficult to find. And in some cases, it may disappear altogether.

CHAPTER 8

The Future of Mental Health Understanding

The Future of Mental Health Understanding

CHAPTER 8

Recovery, Healing, and Reconnection
Introduction: A Shift in Perspective
For decades, mental health has been understood through categories, diagnoses separated into distinct boxes: personality disorders, psychotic disorders, neurocognitive disorders. Each with its own criteria. Each with its own treatment path. Each studied in isolation.

But what if these categories are not as separate as we have believed? What if narcissism, schizophrenia, and dementia are not isolated conditions, but points along a deeper, interconnected continuum of the human mind?

And what if the key to understanding them lies in something we have long dismissed as merely pathological... Fantasy.

This chapter explores the future of mental health through a new lens, one that integrates disciplines, centers compassion, and reframes fantasy not simply as dysfunction, but as a dimension of human cognition that can both heal and harm.

Section I: Integrating What Was Once Separate

1. The Fragmentation of Mental Health Science

Modern mental health systems have been built on specialization:

- Personality disorders studied through behavioral and relational frameworks
- Schizophrenia examined through neurochemical and psychotic models
- Dementia researched through neurodegeneration and aging

Each discipline has advanced significantly, but often without cross-communication.

This has created:

- Diagnostic silos
- Treatment gaps
- Missed opportunities for early intervention

The FDCC model challenges this fragmentation by proposing that:

These conditions share overlapping cognitive, emotional, and neurological pathways.

2. A Continuum-Based Model of Understanding

Rather than viewing disorders as isolated categories, the future of mental health lies in continuum-based frameworks:

- Narcissism → Distortion of self-perception and relational reality
- Schizophrenia → Distortion of external reality and perception
- Dementia → Breakdown of memory, identity, and cognitive structure

Each represents a different point along a shared pathway of:

- Reality distortion
- Identity instability
- Cognitive vulnerability

This integrated view allows clinicians and researchers to:

- Identify early warning signs across conditions

- Develop interventions that address shared mechanisms
- Understand progression rather than isolated symptoms

3. Bridging Psychology and Neuroscience

The future requires a marriage between mind and brain:

- Psychological frameworks explain experience
- Neuroscience explains mechanism

Together, they reveal:

- How repeated thought patterns shape neural pathways
- How emotional trauma influences cognitive processing
- How prolonged distortion can alter brain structure and function

This integration is essential for validating the FDCC theory that:

Long-term immersion in distorted realities may lead to lasting neurological change.

Section II: Compassion-Based Frameworks

1. Moving Beyond Judgment

One of the greatest barriers in mental health is not lack of knowledgebut lack of compassion.

Narcissism is often labeled as:

- Manipulative
- Selfish
- Unchangeable

Schizophrenia is often feared as:

- Dangerous
- Unpredictable
- Detached from reality

Dementia is often seen as:

- A loss of personhood
- An irreversible decline

These perceptions create distance instead of understanding.

But what if we reframed these conditions as:

- Adaptive responses gone too far
- Protective mechanisms that became permanent
- Minds trying to survive in the only way they know how

2. The Role of Empathy in Treatment

Compassion-based care does not excuse harmful behavior—it seeks to understand its origin.

When clinicians, caregivers, and loved ones approach individuals with:

- Curiosity instead of judgment
- Patience instead of frustration
- Presence instead of avoidance

...it creates space for:

- Trust
- Engagement
- Healing

This is particularly critical for individuals who:

- Have experienced chronic invalidation
- Struggle with identity stability
- Rely on fantasy as a coping mechanism

3. Rehumanizing the Diagnosis

At its core, mental health care must return to a simple truth:

Behind every diagnosis is a human being trying to make sense of their world.

Rehumanizing care means:

- Seeing beyond symptoms
- Valuing lived experience
- Recognizing the person beneath the pathology

This shift is not just ethical, it is therapeutically effective.

Section III: Fantasy as a Dimension of Mind

1. Rethinking Fantasy

Traditionally, fantasy has been viewed as:

- Escapism
- Delusion
- Distortion

But fantasy is also:

- Creativity
- Imagination
- Vision

It is a core human capacity.

The problem is not fantasy itself, it is immersion without grounding.

2. The Dual Nature of Fantasy

Fantasy exists on a spectrum:

Adaptive Fantasy	Maladaptive Fantasy
Creative thinking	Delusional belief systems
Goal visualization	Grandiose distortion
Emotional processing	Escape from reality
Innovation	Cognitive entrapment

Healthy fantasy:

- Enhances reality
- Inspires growth
- Supports emotional resilience

Unregulated fantasy:

- Replaces reality
- Distorts identity
- Weakens cognitive anchors

3. Fantasy as a Cognitive Dimension

The FDCC model proposes that fantasy is not just a symptom—it is a dimension of the mind that interacts with:

- Memory
- Identity
- Perception
- Emotion

When balanced, it contributes to:

- Creativity
- Problem-solving
- Meaning-making

When dysregulated, it contributes to:

- Distortion
- Disconnection
- Cognitive decline

4. The Tipping Point: When Fantasy Becomes Reality

The critical shift occurs when:

- Internal narratives override external feedback
- Reality testing weakens
- Memory becomes unreliable

At this point:

- The mind begins to reorganize around distortion
- Identity becomes anchored in fantasy
- Cognitive pathways reinforce the altered reality

This is where the continuum accelerates toward:

- Psychosis
- Identity fragmentation
- Neurocognitive decline

Section IV: Recovery, Healing, and Reconnection

1. Recovery as Reorientation

Recovery is not simply symptom reduction, it is reconnection to reality, self, and others.

This involves:

- Rebuilding cognitive anchors
- Restoring identity coherence
- Strengthening reality testing

Recovery asks:

"What is real?"

"Who am I?"

"Where do I belong?"

2. Healing Through Integration

Healing occurs when fragmented parts of the self are:

- Recognized
- Validated
- Integrated

For individuals along the FDCC continuum, this may involve:

- Reconnecting past and present identity
- Differentiating fantasy from lived experience
- Developing emotional regulation skills

3. The Role of Connection

Isolation fuels distortion.

Connection restores clarity.

Healing is accelerated through:

- Therapeutic relationships
- Supportive communities
- Family engagement

These connections provide:

- External reality anchors
- Emotional safety
- Corrective experiences

4. Rebuilding Identity

At the heart of recovery is identity reconstruction.

This involves:

- Moving beyond labels
- Reclaiming personal narrative
- Establishing a stable sense of self

Identity becomes the anchor that:

- Grounds perception
- Stabilizes memory
- Guides behavior

5. Hope in the Continuum

Even within a model that acknowledges progression toward dementia, there is hope.

Because:

- Not all paths lead to decline
- Not all distortions become permanent
- Not all minds remain lost

With early intervention, compassionate care, and integrated treatment:

- Distortion can be reduced
- Identity can be restored
- Cognitive decline can be slowed, or prevented

Closing Reflection: A New Way Forward

The future of mental health is not in stricter categories, but in deeper understanding.

It is in:

- Integration instead of separation
- Compassion instead of judgment
- Curiosity instead of assumption

And most importantly
It is in recognizing that the human mind is not broken, it is complex.
Fantasy is not the enemy.
Distortion is not the identity.
And no person should be defined solely by their diagnosis.

If we begin to see mental health through this lens,
as a continuum, as a dynamic system, as a deeply human experience,
then we do more than treat conditions.
We restore people.
We reconnect minds.
And we create a future where understanding replaces
misunderstanding, one mind at a time.

CONCLUSION

One Mind, One Continuum

One Mind, One Continuum

CONCLUSION

Throughout this book, we have explored what were once considered separate conditions, narcissism, schizophrenia, and dementia, and uncovered a deeper truth: they may not be isolated diagnoses, but interconnected expressions of how the human mind relates to reality, identity, and memory.

At the center of this work is a simple yet profound realization:
The mind does not break in categories; it shifts along a continuum. From the early stages of adaptive imagination to the depths of cognitive decline, the journey is not defined by labels, but by the degree to which reality becomes distorted, identity becomes unstable, and memory becomes unreliable.

We began by examining narcissism and schizophrenia, two conditions often misunderstood, misdiagnosed, and separated by traditional frameworks. Yet, when viewed through the lens of the Fantasy–Distortion Cognitive Continuum (FDCC Model), their similarities become undeniable. Both involve a reorganization of reality. Both rely on forms of fantasy, whether rooted in identity or perception. And both, when left unaddressed, can lead to deeper cognitive disruption.

As we moved forward, we explored the role of fantasy, not as an enemy, but as a powerful dimension of the mind. Fantasy allows us to dream, to create, to cope.

But when it replaces reality instead of enhancing it, it becomes a trap. A place where the mind can become stuck, reinforcing narratives that distance individuals from truth, from others, and ultimately from themselves.

We then examined how these distortions affect identity, memory, and neurological functioning. The brain does not passively observe these patterns, it adapts to them. Repeated thoughts shape neural pathways. Distorted realities become encoded. Emotional experiences reinforce cognitive patterns.

Over time, what begins as a protective mechanism can become a permanent structure.

This is where the continuum deepens.
Dementia was introduced not simply as a condition of aging, but as a potential endpoint, a "dimension of no return", where the brain loses its ability to reconstruct reality, maintain identity, and preserve memory. Whether reached through neurodegeneration, prolonged cognitive strain, or other factors, it represents a state where the mind can no longer find its way back.

Yet, this book is not a story of inevitability, it is a call to awareness.
Because what determines the outcome is not just the presence of distortion, but the duration, recognition, and response to it.
Misdiagnosis delays understanding.
Lack of intervention reinforces distortion.
Isolation accelerates decline.
But the opposite is also true.
Accurate diagnosis creates clarity.
Early intervention restores direction.
Connection rebuilds reality.

We explored the importance of anchoring individuals back to reality, through therapy, memory reinforcement, neurological care, and most importantly, human connection. Because reality is not only something we perceive, but also something we co-create through relationships, experiences, and shared understanding.

And finally, we looked toward the future.A future where mental health is no longer fragmented into rigid categories, but understood as a dynamic system. A future where compassion replaces judgment.

Where clinicians look beyond symptoms to underlying processes. Where fantasy is not dismissed, but understood as a dimension that must be balanced, not eliminated.

The Final Truth

At its core, this book leaves us with one unifying truth:
The mind becomes what it repeatedly believes.
If it believes in distortion long enough, distortion becomes reality.
If it lives in fantasy long enough, fantasy becomes identity.
And if it loses connection long enough, it may lose its way entirely.
But if guided...
if grounded...
if understood...
The mind can return.

A Closing Reflection

For those who live with these experiences...
For those who love someone navigating them...
For those who work to understand and treat them...

This work is for you.
May it remind you that:

- No mind is simply “broken”
- No diagnosis tells the full story
- And no person is beyond the need for understanding

Because behind every distorted thought is a human trying to make sense of their world.
And sometimes, what they need most is not correction…
but connection.

“When we learn to understand the mind, we don’t just treat disorders, we restore humanity.”- Dr. Kindall M. Bundy

EPILOGUE

When the Mind Whispers Back

When the Mind Whispers Back

EPILOGUE

There is a moment, quiet, almost unnoticeable, when the mind begins to shift.
It doesn't announce itself.
It doesn't ask permission.
It just... begins.
Maybe it starts as a thought you don't question.
A story you tell yourself to make something hurt less.
A version of reality that feels safer than the truth.
And for a while, it works.
You feel stronger.
More in control.
Less vulnerable.
Or maybe
You feel protected.
Disconnected.
Numb enough to survive what once felt unbearable.
The mind is brilliant like that.
It will build entire worlds to keep you from breaking.

But here's the part no one talks about:
At some point...
the world it built for you starts to keep you in.

But here's the part no one talks about:
At some point...
the world it built for you starts to keep you in.

You don't notice it right away.
The stories feel real.
The feelings feel justified.
The distance feels necessary.
And anyone who challenges it?
They don't understand you.
They don't see what you see.
They don't feel what you feel.
So you hold tighter.
To the narrative.
To the identity.
To the version of reality that now feels like the only one that makes sense.

Some people call it narcissism.
Some call it schizophrenia.
Some call it cognitive decline.
But what if...
before it had a name...
before it had a diagnosis...
it was just a mind trying to survive?

A mind trying to make sense of pain.
A mind trying to protect itself from being unseen.
A mind trying to rewrite a story it didn't have the power to change.

And somewhere along the way...
the protection became the prison.

I want you to think about someone.
Not a diagnosis.
Not a label.
A person.
Someone you've struggled to understand.
Someone who hurt you.
Someone who confused you.
Or maybe...
Someone you see when you look in the mirror.

What if their reality isn't something they chose...
but something they slowly adapted to?
What if the distortion you see
is the only way they've learned to stay intact?
What if the silence...
the distance...
the grandiosity...
the confusion...
isn't about control at all...
but survival?

This doesn't excuse the harm.
But it explains the humanity.

Because here is the truth that changes everything:
No one wakes up and chooses to lose their grip on reality.
It happens in layers.
In repetitions.
In moments that slowly reshape the mind.

Until one day...
what is real
and what is constructed
no longer feel different.

And if you've never experienced that...
be grateful.
But don't be quick to judge.

Because the line between grounded and distorted
is not as thick as we pretend it is.
It is thin.
Flexible.
Human.

And that's what this book has been about all along.
Not proving who is right.
Not labeling who is wrong.
But understanding that the mind...
your mind, my mind, every mind...
is constantly balancing between:
Truth
and interpretation
Reality
and protection
Clarity
and distortion

Some people lose that balance.
Some people never had the chance to learn it.
And some people...
are still fighting to find their way back.

So what do we do with this?
We don't turn away.
We don't reduce people to diagnoses.
We don't pretend we are above what we don't understand.

We lean in.
With awareness.
With boundaries.
With compassion.

Because sometimes the most powerful thing you can offer someone
is not correction...
but connection to something real.

A moment of truth.
A consistent presence.
A reminder that reality can be safe too.

And if you are the one reading this...
feeling like parts of your own mind have drifted—
like you've believed things that later didn't make sense...
like you've held onto stories that hurt you...

You are not lost.
You are not broken.
You are human.

And the fact that you can question it,
that you can reflect,
that you can see even a glimpse of the difference—
means something powerful:
You are still connected.

And connection...
is where everything begins again.

So as you close this book, I don't want you to just walk away with knowledge.
I want you to walk away with awareness.
With softness where there used to be judgment.
With curiosity where there used to be confusion.
With understanding where there used to be distance.

Because when we stop asking
"What's wrong with them?"
and start asking
"What happened to their reality?"

We don't just change how we see mental health.
We change how we see people.

And maybe... just maybe
we create a world where fewer minds have to get lost
just to be understood.

“Not every distorted mind is broken, some were just never brought back.”- Dr. Kindall M. Bundy

References

A.

American Psychiatric Association. (2022). Diagnostic and statistical manual of mental disorders (5th ed., text rev.; DSM-5-TR). American Psychiatric Publishing.

American Psychiatric Association. (2013). Diagnostic and statistical manual of mental disorders (5th ed.). American Psychiatric Publishing. https://doi.org/10.1176/appi.books.9780890425596

Andreasen, N. C. (1999). A unitary model of schizophrenia: Bleuler's "fragmented phrene" as schizencephaly. Archives of General Psychiatry, 56(9), 781–787. https://doi.org/10.1001/archpsyc.56.9.781

Andreasen, N. C. (1997). Linking mind and brain in the study of mental illnesses: A project for a scientific psychopathology. Science, 275(5306), 1586–1593. https://doi.org/10.1126/science.275.5306.1586

Arnsten, A. F. T. (2009). Stress signalling pathways that impair prefrontal cortex structure and function. Nature Reviews Neuroscience, 10(6), 410–422. https://doi.org/10.1038/nrn2648

B.

Barch, D. M., & Sheffield, J. M. (2023). Cognitive impairments in schizophrenia: Mechanisms, measurement, and treatment. Annual Review of Clinical Psychology, 19, 417–443. https://doi.org/10.1146/annurev-clinpsy-072220-021444

Beck, A. T., Rector, N. A., Stolar, N., & Grant, P. (2009). Schizophrenia: Cognitive theory, research, and therapy. Guilford Press.

References

Beck, A. T., & Rector, N. A. (2005). Cognitive approaches to schizophrenia: Theory and therapy. Annual Review of Clinical Psychology, 1, 577–606. https://doi.org/10.1146/annurev.clinpsy.1.102803.144154

Beason-Held, L. L., Kraut, M. A., & Resnick, S. M. (2008). Stability of default-mode network activity in the aging brain. Brain Imaging and Behavior, 2(2), 123–131. https://doi.org/10.1007/s11682-008-9023-3

Buckner, R. L., & DiNicola, L. M. (2023). The brain's default network: Updated anatomy, physiology, and evolving insights. Nature Reviews Neuroscience, 24(3), 181–198. https://doi.org/10.1038/s41583-022-00641-5

Buckner, R. L., Andrews-Hanna, J. R., & Schacter, D. L. (2008). The brain's default network: Anatomy, function, and relevance to disease. Annals of the New York Academy of Sciences, 1124(1), 1–38.

Buckner, R. L. (2004). Memory and executive function in aging and dementia. Neuron, 44(1), 195–208. https://doi.org/10.1016/j.neuron.2004.09.006

C.

Caligor, E., Levy, K. N., & Yeomans, F. E. (2015). Narcissistic personality disorder: Diagnostic and clinical challenges. The American Journal of Psychiatry, 172(5), 415–422. https://doi.org/10.1176/appi.ajp.2014.14060723

Campbell, W. K., & Miller, J. D. (Eds.). (2011). The handbook of narcissism and narcissistic personality disorder: Theoretical approaches, empirical findings, and treatments. John Wiley & Sons.

References

Coyle, J. T. (2006). Glutamate and schizophrenia: Beyond the dopamine hypothesis. Cellular and Molecular Neurobiology, 26(4–6), 365–384. https://doi.org/10.1007/s10571-006-9062-8

F.

Frith, C. D. (1992). The cognitive neuropsychology of schizophrenia. Lawrence Erlbaum Associates.

Fonagy, P., Luyten, P., Allison, E., & Campbell, C. (2023). Mentalizing, epistemic trust, and the phenomenology of personality disorders. The Lancet Psychiatry, 10(2), 120–132. https://doi.org/10.1016/S2215-0366(22)00379-9

Frisoni, G. B., Altomare, D., Thal, D. R., Ribaldi, F., van der Kant, R., Ossenkoppele, R., Blennow, K., Cummings, J., & Scheltens, P. (2023). The probabilistic model of Alzheimer disease: The amyloid–tau–neurodegeneration (ATN) framework. Nature Reviews Neurology, 19(2), 91–106. https://doi.org/10.1038/s41582-022-00749-8

G.

Gerrans, P. (2014). Pathologies of hyperfamiliarity and hyper-salience: Toward a unified account of delusions. Review of Philosophy and Psychology, 5(1), 1–19. https://doi.org/10.1007/s13164-013-0156-1

Goff, D. C., & Coyle, J. T. (2001). The emerging role of glutamate in the pathophysiology and treatment of schizophrenia. American Journal of Psychiatry, 158(9), 1367–1377. https://doi.org/10.1176/appi.ajp.158.9.1367

H.

Hare, T. A., & Camerer, C. F. (2023). Self-control and valuation in the prefrontal cortex: Implications for decision-making and identity regulation. Neuron, 111(5), 685–699. https://doi.org/10.1016/j.neuron.2023.01.012

References

Heckers, S., Barch, D. M., Bustillo, J., Gaebel, W., Gur, R., Malaspina, D., Owen, M. J., Schultz, S., Tandon, R., Tsuang, M., Van Os, J., & Carpenter, W. (2013). Structure of the psychotic disorders classification in DSM-5. Schizophrenia Research, 150(1), 11–14. https://doi.org/10.1016/j.schres.2013.04.039

I.

Insel, T. R. (2023). Rethinking schizophrenia: A path forward for diagnosis and treatment. JAMA Psychiatry, 80(4), 305–306. https://doi.org/10.1001/jamapsychiatry.2023.0123

J.

Jack, C. R., Jr., Bennett, D. A., Blennow, K., Carrillo, M. C., Dunn, B., Haeberlein, S. B., Holtzman, D. M., Jagust, W., Jessen, F., Karlawish, J., Liu, E., Molinuevo, J. L., Montine, T., Phelps, C., Rankin, K. P., Rowe, C. C., Scheltens, P., Siemers, E., Snyder, H. M., & Sperling, R. (2024). NIA-AA research framework: Toward a biological definition of Alzheimer's disease (update). Alzheimer's & Dementia, 20(1), 1–15. https://doi.org/10.1002/alz.13000

Jack, C. R., Jr., Knopman, D. S., Jagust, W. J., Shaw, L. M., Aisen, P. S., Weiner, M. W., Petersen, R. C., & Trojanowski, J. Q. (2010). Hypothetical model of dynamic biomarkers of the Alzheimer's pathological cascade. The Lancet Neurology, 9(1), 119–128. https://doi.org/10.1016/S1474-4422(09)70299-6

K.

Kernberg, O. F. (2016). What is personality? Journal of Personality Disorders, 30(2), 145–156. https://doi.org/10.1521/pedi.2016.30.2.145

Kernberg, O. F. (1975). Borderline conditions and pathological narcissism. Jason Aronson.

References

Klinger, E. (2009). Daydreaming and fantasizing: Thought flow and motivation. In K. D. Markman, W. M. P. Klein, & J. A. Suhr (Eds.), Handbook of imagination and mental simulation (pp. 225–239). Psychology Press.

Krause, N., & Bastida, E. (2011). Religion, suffering, and health among older Mexican Americans. Journal of Aging Studies, 25(2), 171–180. https://doi.org/10.1016/j.jaging.2010.08.013

M.

Menon, V. (2011). Large-scale brain networks and psychopathology: A unifying triple network model. Trends in Cognitive Sciences, 15(10), 483–506. https://doi.org/10.1016/j.tics.2011.08.003

Mesulam, M. M. (2000). Principles of behavioral and cognitive neurology (2nd ed.). Oxford University Press.

McAdams, D. P. (2001). The psychology of life stories. Review of General Psychology, 5(2), 100–122. https://doi.org/10.1037/1089-2680.5.2.100

McKhann, G. M., Knopman, D. S., Chertkow, H., Hyman, B. T., Jack, C. R., Jr., Kawas, C. H., Klunk, W. E., Koroshetz, W. J., Manly, J. J., Mayeux, R., Mohs, R. C., Morris, J. C., Rossor, M. N., Scheltens, P., Carrillo, M. C., Thies, B., Weintraub, S., & Phelps, C. H. (2011). The diagnosis of dementia due to Alzheimer's disease: Recommendations from the National Institute on Aging–Alzheimer's Association workgroups. Alzheimer's & Dementia, 7(3), 263–269. https://doi.org/10.1016/j.jalz.2011.03.005

References

Miller, B. L., & Seeley, W. W. (2023). Frontotemporal dementia: Clinical features and pathophysiology. The Lancet Neurology, 22(1), 82–97. https://doi.org/10.1016/S1474-4422(22)00365-9

Murray, R. M., Bhavsar, V., Tripoli, G., & Howes, O. (2017). 30 years on: How the neurodevelopmental hypothesis of schizophrenia morphed into the developmental risk factor model of psychosis. Schizophrenia Bulletin, 43(6), 1190–1196.

N.

Neff, K. D., & Germer, C. K. (2022). The mindful self-compassion workbook (2nd ed.). Guilford Press.

P.

Panksepp, J. (1998). Affective neuroscience: The foundations of human and animal emotions. Oxford University Press.
37/0003-066X.54.3.182

Pincus, A. L., & Lukowitsky, M. R. (2010). Pathological narcissism and narcissistic personality disorder. Annual Review of Clinical Psychology, 6(1), 421–446.
https://doi.org/10.1146/annurev.clinpsy.121208.131215

R

Raichle, M. E. (2015). The brain's default mode network. Annual Review of Neuroscience, 38, 433–447.
https://doi.org/10.1146/annurev-neuro-071013-014030

Ridgeway, B., & Correll, C. U. (2017). Neurobiology of schizophrenia: A focus on neural circuits and neurotransmitters. Psychiatric Clinics of North America, 40(3), 359–372.
https://doi.org/10.1016/j.psc.2017.05.004

References

Rosenhan, D. L., & Seligman, M. E. P. (1989). Abnormal psychology (2nd ed.). W. W. Norton & Company.

S.

Schacter, D. L. (1999). The seven sins of memory: Insights from psychology and cognitive neuroscience. American Psychologist, 54(3), 182–203. https://doi.org/10.10

Sheffield, J. M., & Barch, D. M. (2024). Cognition and functional outcomes in schizophrenia: Advances and future directions. Biological Psychiatry, 95(2), 120–132. https://doi.org/10.1016/j.biopsych.2023.05.015

Sedikides, C., & Gregg, A. P. (2008). Self-enhancement: Food for thought. Perspectives on Psychological Science, 3(2), 102–116. https://doi.org/10.1111/j.1745-6916.2008.00068.x

Singer, J. L. (2004). Imagination and daydreaming: A call for research. Routledge.

Squire, L. R., & Wixted, J. T. (2011). The cognitive neuroscience of human memory since H.M. Annual Review of Neuroscience, 34, 259–288. https://doi.org/10.1146/annurev-neuro-061010-113720

T.

Taylor, S. E., Pham, L. B., Rivkin, I. D., & Armor, D. A. (1998). Harnessing the imagination: Mental simulation, self-regulation, and coping. American Psychologist, 53(4), 429–439. https://doi.org/10.1037/0003-066X.53.4.429

References

U.

Uddin, L. Q. (2015). Salience processing and insular cortical function and dysfunction. Nature Reviews Neuroscience, 16(1), 55–61. https://doi.org/10.1038/nrn3857

V.

van der Meer, L., de Vos, A. E., Stiekema, A. P. M., Pijnenborg, G. H. M., & Aleman, A. (2023). Insight in schizophrenia: A neurocognitive and neurobiological perspective. Neuroscience & Biobehavioral Reviews, 144, 104965. https://doi.org/10.1016/j.neubiorev.2023.104965

van der Meer, L., Costafreda, S., Aleman, A., & David, A. S. (2010). Self-reflection and the brain: A theoretical review and meta-analysis of neuroimaging studies with implications for schizophrenia. Neuroscience & Biobehavioral Reviews, 34(6), 935–946.

W.

Waters, F., Woodward, T., Allen, P., Aleman, A., & Sommer, I. (2012). Self-recognition deficits in schizophrenia patients with auditory hallucinations: A meta-analysis of the literature. Schizophrenia Bulletin, 38(4), 741–750. https://doi.org/10.1093/schbul/sbq144

World Health Organization. (2023). Dementia: Key facts and global health estimates. https://www.who.int/news-room/fact-sheets/detail/dementia

World Health Organization. (2019). International classification of diseases for mortality and morbidity statistics (11th Revision).

Made in the USA
Monee, IL
21 April 2026

48720291R00079